HISTORICAL COMPUTER LANGUAGES VOLUME IV: Assembly Language (ASM) Programming

by

Dr. Peta Trigger Ph.D, Ed.D

K B P

2 Emms Hill Barns
Hamsterley
County Durham
First published 2014

ISBN 9781495399220
PRINTED BY CREATESPACE
https://www.createspace.com

FOREWORD

This volume, the final volume of the series about computer programming in historical languages entitled *Historical Computing*, describes the stages involved in the writing of an assembly language program for the Z80 microprocessor, executed from mid- 1970's - 1980's *BASIC,* the programming language fully explored in Volumes I-III, running on a 1981 *Research Machines 380 Z* micro-computer.

The purpose of the program is to display a circle in graphics, of a size such that it consists of some 300 points, fast enough to give the impression of movement when plotted in one position in white, 'erased' by plotting it in black, plotting it in white again at some new position. This circle graphic was to be part of a pedagogic program written in *BASIC* in *Research Machines 380Z* and *Apple II* micro-computer versions to teach fraction concepts using dynamic computer graphics- the circle being one of the three 'whole' shapes used in the program. The program was developed and tested in the early 1980's as part of the author's Ph.D research, with the *Research Machines 380Z* and *Apple II* then beginning to come into general use in educational institutions. Some of the results obtained feature in examples of the use of the non-parametric tests programmed in *BASIC* described in Volume II of this series. Plotting the circle directly in *BASIC* was found to be too slow, and so an assembly language program was written to plot the points of the circle, which was then translated into machine code and executed from the *BASIC* pedagogic program. All the steps involved in this process are explained in in the text.

The layout of this volume is as follows. The structure of the Z80 microprocessor- the heart of the *Research Machines 380Z* microcomputer on which all the programming was done, is first considered, followed by the operation of its main features. Next, the lexicon (the naming of the instructions, known as 'mnemonics') and syntax (the rules for combining these instructions) of *ZASM* Assembly Language (ASM) are described, and how they are used to write a program to produce graphics, using the "PLOT" subroutine in *BASIC* (this is in the file 'basicsg2' loaded into computer memory from disc at the CP/M prompt) on the *Research Machines 380Z* microcomputer.

4

This is followed by a consideration of the binary codes for the ASM mnemonics and operands, and their conversion into hexadecimal numbers suitable for insertion into the 380Z's memory.

The final machine code program is the result of writing, testing and debugging several simpler but increasingly complex programs beginning with the plotting of a single graphics point, and in subsequent programs progressively adding sequences of instructions to produce a full circle of graphics points; to produce parts of circles (arcs) as well as full circles; to produce circles and arcs with user-defined starting and finishing points; and finally to produce circles and arcs with user-defined starting and finishing points with user-defined centre co-ordinates. (The radius of the circle is fixed).

The 'book-keeping' aspects of the work, including choice of locations in 380Z memory for the machine code program, the creation of data files for the screen positions of the graphics points to be plotted, inserting the machine code program into the 380Z's memory, and calling the machine code program from and returning to *BASIC* on the *380Z*, are covered. Finally, the use of the machine code program in generating the moving (or rather creating the illusion of moving) graphics shapes used in the pedagogic program is described, showing how the data, pokes and circle subroutine components of the machine language programming work and fit into the organisation of the *BASIC* pedagogic program, and how the programming techniques described in the text were used within it.

TABLE OF CONTENTS

8

12

LIST OF FIGURES

14

LIST OF TABLES

16

LIST OF EXAMPLES

LIST OF PRINT-OUTS

18

LIST OF PLATES

CHAPTER 1 : INTRODUCTION

In computer programming the direct graphics plotting of shapes in *BASIC* for use in a dynamic pedagogic program to teach basic fractions, it was found that execution was too slow. Circles of the size required, with a diameter a substantial part of the entire screen width, consist of over 300 graphics 'dots'. The position of each dot has first to be calculated using sine and cosine functions, scaled and then plotted. Even though the dot positions calculated for one quadrant are sufficient to determine the dot positions in the remaining three quadrants by adding or subtracting from a constant, speeding up execution time, it was found that plotting a full circle took many seconds. This meant that circles plotted in *BASIC* could not be used in the pedagogic program which translated, rotated and 'flashed' shapes on the computer screen because the movement effected was too slow.

The problem with using *BASIC* for this purpose is that though easy to use, it is a 'high level' computing language. A low level program, though harder to use would enable much faster instruction execution and so it was decided to write a program in Assembly Language (ASM) to plot a full circle or circle arcs, which when translated into machine code, could be "CALL"-ed from *BASIC* to execute it. This program was found to produce a full graphics circle of radius 50 in under a second, and used with suitable delay loops if necessary, circles and circle arcs could be moved around the computer screen at the desired speed for such pedagogic purposes as showing division of a whole into parts and comparing their sizes.

The pedagogic program was to be used with the *Research Machines 380Z* microcomputer running basicsg2, beginning to come into use schools. The *380Z*, as is implied, is based on the *Zilog Z80* microprocessor CPU. Hence the first stage in writing the machine program was to study the organisation of the *Z80* microprocessor- for example its accumulator & registers and memory & stack.

The second stage was to study the Assembly Language of the *Z80*, ZASM, more particularly those 'mnemonics' which would be obviously necessary in writing the program- for example instructions manipulating operands and addresses on the stack, instructions for storing and manipulating operands in the accumulator and register, for performing simple arithmetical addition and multiplication operations, for moving to and from the machine code program from and to the *BASIC* program, and so on.

The third stage was to write the ASM program, consisting of mnemonic instructions, together with suitable operand values chosen according to the memory locations available for use in the 380Z memory and the address of the "PLOT" subroutine in basicsg2 used to plot each 'dot' of the circle.

The fourth stage was to learn how to translate the mnemonics of the ASM program into binary and then hexadecimal codes which could be inserted into the *380Z*'s memory.

The fifth stage consisted of several steps beginning with a simple program plotting a single point, progressing onto a more complex program plotting a full circle only with centre in a fixed screen position, and ultimately a program which would plot a part of a circle of the desired arc length in the desired position on the computer screen.

At each step in this fifth stage, the binary codes for the ASM mnemonic instructions had to be 'looked up' from the *Z80* instruction list. Then, these binary values were converted into hexadecimal values which would be put into *380Z* memory. Furthermore, the address of starting point for the machine code program in *380Z* memory had to be determined and a 'block' of memory allocated and cleared ready for use. Having done this, the starting address of the machine code program could be CALL-ed from *BASIC* and executed, a final return instruction returning control to *BASIC* after plotting the lastl point.

Once the machine program had been de-bugged, the sixth and final stage was to investigate the use of program instructions in *BASIC* in order to 'draw' the circle sectors representing 1/2s, 1/3s, 1/4s and 1/10s used in the pedagogic program, at any screen position and in any orientation. Algorithms in *BASIC* also had to be created to produce the illusion of movement of shapes around the screen, rotation of shapes and 'flashing' (highlighting by 'switching' a shape on and off), which were important pedagogic devices used in the teaching program.

Again, the work was broken down into steps progressing from the simple to the complex. The other whole shapes used in the pedagogic program were a square of side 100 screen positions ('pixels') and a rectangle of length 100 and height. These shapes were easier to deal with than the circle, and both could be 'drawn' in graphics using the subroutines 'built-in' to basicsg2 on the *380Z*. These, like the "CIRCLE" (*sic*) machine code subroutine written by the author, could be CALL-ed from *BASIC* using the built-in names "PLOT" and "LINE" supplied with appropriate arguments for intensity, position and line length. In the first step in this final stage a start was made with squares and square parts, because these were easiest to program having equal length sides. Having identified various programming techniques and algorithms which could be successfully used with the square, these could be adapted for use with the slightly more complex (to program) rectangle. Finally, the knowledge and experience gained from these first two steps was applied to programming circles and circle parts (whole circles, sectors and 'slices' (circle arcs and chords)).

The ultimate result of all this work was that a portfolio of programming techniques, algorithms and subroutines became available which enabled the author to draw any desired part or whole circle, square, thin rectangle or rod in any shade, orientation and position on the computer screen, and to rotate, translate and to 'flash' any of these shapes through any desired angle and distance at any desired speed, thereby giving the author a suitably versatile graphics-shape drawing 'toolbox' which could be used in designing the pedagogic program.

CHAPTER 2: Z80 ARCHITECTURE

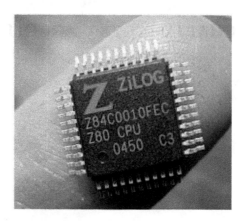

The *Z80* microprocessor is shown above. It is the central processing unit (CPU) of the *Research Machines 380Z* microcomputer which is shown below, which was used in developing the machine code program described here:

The Research Machines 380Z Micro-Computer
The other principal components of the computer
system, which can be seen in the photo,

are the monitor or visual display unit (VDU) with screen (shown separately in the photo above), disc drives and keyboard. The main features of the *Z80* used in the development of the machine code program will now be described.

THE REGISTERS

The *Z80* has six 8-bit (or single *byte*) registers, denoted by 'B', 'C', 'D', 'E', 'H' and 'L', and six auxiliary registers denoted by 'B"', 'C"', 'D"', 'E"', 'H"' and 'L"' which are used to store data temporarily whilst it is being manipulated, for example whilst it is being used in arithmetical or logical operations.

The auxiliary registers may be used in exactly the

same way, and can save a considerable amount of shifting data in and out of registers into and out of memory. A simple instruction transfers control from one set to the other and back. These single registers may be combined in the pairs 'BC', 'DE' and 'HL' for use in 16-bit operations. 8-bit operations involve numbers up to 255 decimal, i.e., 2^8 -1 (255D), since the left-most bit has the value 2^7 D and the right-most bit 2^0. 16-bit (2 byte) operations therefore involve numbers up to 65535 which is 2^{16} -1 (65535 D). The lowest 8 bits of the number (the low byte) are stored in the register pairs first, followed by the highest 8 bits (the high byte). The diagram on page 32 summarises this information.

Programming is usually simplified if single registers are used, which can be done when the result of operations using the registers is 255 or less. But 255 in the context of computer programming is very small, and the author found that much of the work in the program described here involved higher numbers. For example, a full circle plotted by the program consisted of 1024 addresses (the locations in the *380Z*'s memory) for the X and Y co-ordinates of the points. And the memory locations addressed in the program ran from hexadecimal 35B8 upwards (denary-hexadecimal conversion is covered later) or 13572 D. Hence, pairs of registers had often to be used.

Main Set		Auxiliary Set	
8 bits	8 bits	8 bits	8 bits
B	C	B'	C'
D	E	D'	E'
H	L	H'	L'

16 bits	16 bits
B C	B'C'
D E	D'E'
H L	H'L'

Single and Paired Registers of the Z80

However, where the low or high byte of a 16-bit number only was to be used in an operation, and for operations such as counting the number times a sequence of instructions was executed (e.g. in counting from 3 down to 0 in multiplying a number by 2 three times to achieve an end result of multiplication by 8 D), the single registers could be used.

THE ACCUMULATOR

The accumulator denoted by A, is more versatile as a single register than the above sets of registers and there is also an auxiliary accumulator A'. It is used to perform 8-bit arithmetical and logical operations:

```
        Main          Auxiliary
    ⌒‿‿‿‿‿‿‿⌒     ⌒‿‿‿‿‿‿‿⌒

      8 bits          8 bits
    ┌───────────┬──────────────┐
    │Accumulator ║ Accumulator │
    │     A     ║      A'      │
    └───────────┴──────────────┘
```

Accumulator Registers of the Z80

For example, addition in the *Z80* must be carried out by first loading one number in the accumulator and then adding a second number to it, the result being contained in the accumulator. Logical operations using the accumulator are not used here.

PROGRAM COUNTER

The program counter register, know as 'PC', is 16 bits wide and keeps account of the whereabouts in memory of the next instruction to be executed. Instructions may be 1-4 bytes long. A 4 byte instruction, for example, will cause the program counter to be incremented 4 times, ready to point to the next instruction. By means of this facility, instructions may be executed out of sequence. For example, the contents of a register may be tested for zero and if this test is positive, a JP (mnemonically JumP) instruction may be used to continue program execution at some other memory location than the next one. In this case, the program counter is incremented or decremented automatically to point to the memory location specified with the JP instruction.

STACK POINTER

The stack pointer register SP is another counting register like the PC register which keeps account of the memory address (location in memory) of the top of the *stack* a special area of memory used for temporary storage and exchange of data. The stack pointer always points to the top of the stack. If the stack is empty, the stack pointer will point to the memory location of this memory location *minus 2*. An instruction can be used to load the stack pointer with a number which sets the address of the bottom of the stack. Each time a datum is added to the stack the stack pointer is incremented by 2. This is explained below.

THE STACK

The stack is a 16-bit area of memory, but data may only be added or removed from the top of the stack. Low memory addresses are towards the top of the stack, high memory addresses towards the bottom. The bottom of the stack therefore contains the *first* 2-byte datum to be added to the stack, and the top of the stack contains the most recently added or *last* datum added. So the last datum which was stored is the first to be retrieved when an instruction is executed to remove a datum from the stack, and the first item stored is the last to be retrieved. This system is known as 'Last in First Out' or 'LIFO'. The stack's structure is shown below.

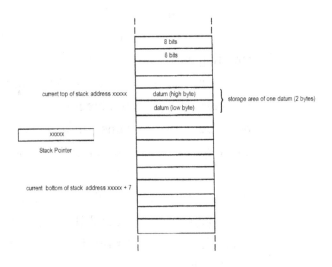

Organisation of the Stack

FLAG REGISTER

The flag register, F, has 8 bits and each bit is assigned a separate function. Numbering of the F bits is left-to-right 0 to 7. The bits used here are bit 1, the zero flag Z and bit 0, the carry flag C. The zero flag is set to 1 if the result of the previous operation is 0. If the result is non-zero, it is reset to 0. A *carry* occurs when the result of an operation is too large to be contained in a register or register pair, requiring an 'extra bit' to store the result. This extra bit goes into the carry flag. For example, suppose the result of an operation in the accumulator results in 257 B. This is $2^8 +1$ D, and so requires 9 bits to store it. The most significant bit (the 9th) value sets the Carry flag to 1. The relevant features of the flag register is below.

```
Bit       0   1   2   3   4   5   6   7
        ┌───┬───┬───┬───┬───┬───┬───┬───┐
        │   │ Z │   │   │   │   │   │ C │
        └───┴───┴───┴───┴───┴───┴───┴───┘
```

Bit 1 is the Zero flag

Bit 7 is the Carry flag

The Flag Register

CHAPTER 3 *ZASM* ASSEMBLY LANGUAGE

MNEMONICS

Assembly language enables a program to written initially without memory addresses and instruction codes which complicate programming considerably. Instead of instruction codes *mnemonics* for semi-English words are used, (for example the JumP instruction referred to above) and instead of memory addresses *labels* are used.

Mnemonics consist of abbreviations for instructions of 2-4 characters long. Each mnemonic is followed in most cases by an operation. Examples are: LD for 'LoaD'- e.g. LD A, where A is the operation, means 'load the accumulator' (with a number or the contents of a register); INC for 'INCrement' - e.g. INC HL means ' increase the contents of the register pair HL by 1'; CP for 'ComPare'- e.g. CP 3A means 'Compare the contents of the accumulator with the number 3A (a hexadecimal number equivalent to 3 x 16 =48 D: hexadecimal numbers are explained in Chapter 6).

As can be seen from the above examples, *operands* may follow the operation which can be registers or numbers (numbers may refer to data values or addresses). Not all mnemonics require an operand or even an operation to be specified, however. For example, 'EXX' (EXchange registers) is used without a specified operation or operand to switch between the use of main and auxiliary registers and vice versa. This is because the operation is implicit in the command 'interchange main and aux regs', and so an operand is not required.

ADDRESSING MODES

Addressing may be *immediate* or *extended*. In the immediate mode, the operation is carried out directly on the operand. In the extended mode, the operand is treated as an address at which the contents of that memory location are to be used in the operation.

The above examples all use the *immediate* addressing mode. In ASM, when an operation is to be carried out in extended mode, it is enclosed in brackets. For example: LD (HL) means load the contents at the memory location stored in the register pair HL, not the contents of HL itself which would require the mnemonic LD HL. More examples of extended addressing mode are given in the next section.

MNEMONIC CODES USED

A description of the mnemonic codes used here in the finished program follows, each with an example and an explanation.

LOAD COMMANDS

1. LD r_1, r_2 where r stands for a single register. E.g.:

LD A,L : replace the existing contents of the accumulator with the contents of register L.

2. LD A, $(n_1 n_2)$. E.g.:

LD A, (7D10): replace the contents of the accumulator with the contents of the *address* 7D10.

3. LD A, (HL): replace the contents of the accumulator with the contents of the *address* in HL.

4. LD $(n_1 n_2)$, A: replace the contents of memory location $n_1 n_2$ with the contents of the accumulator. E.g.:

LD (7B06), A: replace the existing contents of memory location 7B06 with the contents of the accumulator.

5. LD r_ar_b,n_1n_2 where r_ar_b stands for a register pair and n_1n_2 a two byte number, low byte first. E.g.:
LD HL, 37, 65 : replace the existing contents of the HL register pair with 6570. This might data or an address.

6. LD $r_ar_b,(n_1n_2)$ where r_ar_b stands for a register pair and (n_1n_2) a two byte *address*, low byte first. E.g.:
LD BC, (7D16): replace the contents of register pair DE with the contents of memory location 7D16 and 7D17.

7. LD (n_1n_2), HL: replace the contents of memory locations n_1n_2 and $n_1n_2 + 1$ with the contents of register pair HL (the contents of L going into n_1n_2 and the contents of H going into $n_1n_2 + 1$).

ARITHMETIC ADDITION
8. ADC,r: add the contents of register r to the contents in the accumulator, leaving the result in the accumulator. E.g.:

ADC, B: add the contents of the B register to the contents of the accumulator leaving the result in the accumulator.

9. ADD A, (HL): add the contents of the *address* in HL to the contents of the accumulator and leave the result in the accumulator.

10. ADD HL, $r_a r_b$: add the contents of the register pair HL to the contents of the register pair $r_a r_b$ and leave the result in HL. E.g.:

ADD HL, DE: add the contents of register pair HL to the contents of the register pair DE and leave the result in HL.

LOGIC COMMANDS
11. INC r: add 1 to the contents of register r. E.g.:
INC C: add 1 to the contents of C register.

12. INC $r_a r_b$: add 1 to the contents of register pair $r_a r_b$. E.g.:

INC HL: add 1 to the contents of register pair HL.

13. DEC r: subtract 1 from the contents of register r and set the Zero flag according to the result (i.e. to

1 if the result of the operation is zero or 0 if the result is non-zero).

14. CP r: subtract the contents of register r from the contents of the accumulator. Set the Z flag accordingly. E.g.:

CP C: subtract the contents of register C from the contents of the accumulator. Set the Z flag according to the result.

15. CP (HL): subtract the contents of the address in HL from the contents of the accumulator. Set the Z flag according to the result.

16. CP, n: subtract the number n from the contents of the accumulator. Set the Z flag according to the result. E.g.:

CP 128 D: subtract 128 D from the contents of the accumulator and set the Z flag to 1 if the result is 0 or to 0 if the result is non-zero.

17. SLA r: shift the bits of the contents of register r one place to the left. Set the Carry flag to erstwhile bit 7. Set bit 0 to 0. Set the Zero flag according to the result.

E.g.:

SLA L: shift the bits of the contents of register L one place to the left. Set the Carry flag to erstwhile bit 7. Set bit 0 to 0. Set the Zero flag according to the result

CONTROL INSTRUCTIONS

18. JP, n: jump to the address n to execute the next instruction (loads PC register with n). E.g.:

JP, 13752 D: jump to address 13752 D to execute the next instruction.

19. JR Z, n: if the Z flag is set to 1, jump to memory location specified by n., remembering that PC is incremented by 2 *prior* to the addition of n. E.g.1:

JR Z, 13 D: if the Z flag is set to 1, jump to memory location +11 from current memory location.
E.g. 2:

JR Z, -7 D: if the Z flag is set to 1, jump to memory location -5 from current memory location.

20. JR NZ, n: if the Z flag is set to 1, jump to memory location specified by n., remembering that PC is incremented by 2 *prior* to the addition of n. E.g.1:

JR Z, 17 D: if the Z flag is set to 1, jump to memory location +19 from current memory location.
E.g. 2:

JR Z, -12 D: if the Z flag is set to 1, jump to memory location -10 from current memory location.

STACK INSTRUCTIONS

21. PUSH $r_a r_b$: load the contents of register pair $r_a r_b$ into the two consecutive addresses at the top of the stack. The contents of r_a go into the contents of the address SP-1, into SP-2. E.g.:
PUSH HL: load the contents of register pair HL into the two consecutive addresses at the top of the stack. The contents of H go into the contents of the address SP-1, L into SP-2.

22. POP $r_a r_b$: remove the contents of the two consecutive addresses at the top of the stack into register pair $r_a r_b$. The contents of address SP go into

r_a , SP-1 into r_b . E.g.:

POP HL: remove the contents of address SP into H
and SP-1 into L.

4. WRITING THE ASSEMBLY LANGUAGE PROGRAM

An assembly language (ASM) program consists of lines of single operations together with their operands. A line may have a *label* which in the ASM program is used in place of the address of the instruction in the line which is put in when the ASM program is converted into machine code. There are up 4 columns (or 'fields') in each line: a column for the label , a column for the mnemonic operation, a column for the operand and a comment. The comment, which is used to describe the action carried out by the instruction on that line, is separated from the rest of the line by a semi-colon. For example, one line in an ASM program might be:

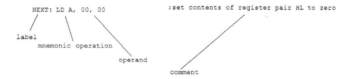

An ASM Program Statement

EXAMPLE PROGRAMS

To illustrate the use of the features of ASM which will be used in writing the graphics program, examples of simpler programs based on the addition of two single byte numbers whose sum occupies a single byte, which successively add in new features, will be described, beginning with simple addition:

```
LD HL, 63 D            ;load register pair HL with 63 D

LD BC, 45 D            ;load the register pair BC with 45 D

ADD HL,BC              ;add the contents of BC =45 to the contents of
                       HL=63 D. Result of 63+45 D is in HL
```

PROGRAM 1: SIMPLE ADDITION OF TWO NUMBERS

```
                       ;63 D is in memory location address 32000 D,
                       ;45 D is in 32003 D.

                       ;the contents of 32001 D, 32003 D, H and B have
                       ;been previously set to 0.

LD HL, (32000 D)       ;load the contents of address 32000 D=63 D and
                       32001 D =0 into HL

LD DE, (32003 D)       ;load the contents of address 32003 D=45 D and
                       32004 D=0 into HL

ADD HL,BC              ;add the contents of BC=45 D to the contents of
                       ;HL=63D

                       ;result is in HL
```

PROGRAM 2: The Numbers to be Added are in Memory

;63 D is in address SP-1. 0 is in address SP-2 and
;address SP-4. 45 D is in address SP-3

POP HL   ;remove 63 D from address SP-1 and 0 from
                          ;address SP-2 and load it into HL

POP BC   ;remove 63 D from address SP-3 and 0 from
                          ;address SP-4 and load it into BC

ADD HL,BC   ;add 45 D in BC to 63 D in HL

                          ;result is in HL

PROGRAM 3: The Numbers to be Added are on the Stack

                          ;63 D is in L, 45 D in C

LD A,L   ;load A with the contents of L=63 D

CP 0   ;subtract 0 from the contents of A, i.e., 63 D - 0,
                          ;which is non-zero and so Z flag is set=0

JR Z, FINISH   ;if the Z flag is set=1, finish. Otherwise continue.

LD A,C   ;load A with the contents of C=45 D

CP 0   ;subtract 0 from the contents of A, i.e., 45 D - 0,
                          ;which is non-zero and so Z flag is set=0

JR Z, FINISH   ;if the Z flag is set=1, finish. Otherwise continue.

ADD A,L   ;add the contents of L=63 D to the contents of
                          ;A=45 D

                          ;result is in A

FINISH

PROGRAM 4: The Numbers to be Added are tested for zero. If either is zero, the Addition
Operation is aborted

	;63 D is in L, 45 D in C.
LD A,L	;load A with the contents of L=63 D
CP 0	;subtract 0 from the contents of A, i.e., 63 D - 0, ;which is non-zero and so Z flag is set=0
JR Z, FINISH	;if the Z flag is set=1, finish. Otherwise continue.
LD A,C	;load A with the contents of C=45 D
CP 0	;subtract 0 from the contents of A, i.e., 45 D - 0, ;which is non-zero and so Z flag is set=0
JR Z, FINISH	;if the Z flag is set=1, finish. Otherwise continue.
LD H,0	;set contents of H to 0
LD B,0	;set contents of B to 0
PUSH HL	;temporarily store contents of HL=63 D in stack
LD L,0	;set contents of L to 0
LD D,3	;D is used as counter
NEXT1: ADD HL,BC	;add 45 D in BC to contents in HL

DEC D	;decrease contents of D by 1. Z flag is set to 1 if ;D=0
JR NZ, NEXT1	;if Z flag is 0 add contents of BC to the contents of ;HL again
	; 3x45 D are in HL
POP BC	;remove contents of stack top (in SP-1) into BC ;=63 D
PUSH HL	;temporarily store contents of HL=3x45 D in stack
LD HL,0	;set contents of HL to 0
LD D,3	;D is used as counter
NEXT2: ADD HL,BC	;add 63 D in BC to contents in HL
DEC D	;decrease contents of D by 1. Z flag is set to 1 if ;D=0
JR NZ, NEXT2	;if Z flag is 0 add contents of BC to the contents of ;HL again
	; 3x63 D are in HL
POP BC	;remove contents of stack top (SP-1) into BC= ;3x45 D
ADD HL,BC	;add the contents of BC=3x45 D to the contents of ;HL=3x63 D
	;result is in HL
FINISH	

PROGRAM 5: Including a Loop to Multiply Numbers by 3 before Adding

	;63 D is in L and C, 45 D in L' and C'. Numbers
	;have been previously checked for zero
EXX	;aux regs
LD D,1	;set contents of D' to 2
EXX	;main regs
START: LD HL,0	;set contents of HL to 0
LD B,0	;set contents of B to 0
LD D,3	;set counter to 3
NEXT: ADD HL,BC	;add 45 D in BC to contents of HL
DEC D	;decrease contents of D by 1. Set Z=0 if D=0
JR Z,NEXT	;if Z=0 add contents of BC to HL again
	;3 x 45 D is in HL
EXX	;use aux. regs
DEC D	;decrease contents of D' by 1
JR Z,CONT	; if Z=0, jump to CONT
JP,START	;to multiply 63 D' in BC by 3
CONT:PUSH HL	;temporarily store contents of HL' = 3x63 D in stack
EXX	;main regs
POP BC	;remove contents of stack top (SP-1) into BC
ADD HL,BC	;add the contents of BC=3x63 D to the contents of
	HL=3x45 D
	;result is in HL

PROGRAM 6: Using the Auxiliary Registers

5. CODING ASSEMBLY LANGUAGE IN BINARY

Referring to Appendix 1, which shows the *Z80* instruction code for each ASM mnemonic operation, it will be seen that these, together with their operands are all in binary. The first step in converting the ASM into a machine program which can be executed by the *Z80* is therefore to convert the ASM mnemonics (op. codes) and operands (nn) in each ASM statement into their binary form. Notice that all op. codes and operands are 8-bit numbers.

CONVERTING DENARY OPERANDS TO BINARY

Appendix 2 contains a table which converts denary numbers into their 8-bit binary equivalent. For example, in the ASM programs in the previous chapter, the two operands 63 D and 45 D were used. From Appendix 2, 63 D is 0011 1111 B and 45 D is 0010 1101 B. Suppose that 63 D is to be loaded into register HL, 45 D into BC prior to adding these two numbers together in HL (Example 1 in Ch. 4). The ASM instructions for accomplishing this are:

LD HL, 63 D

LD BC, 45 D

The instruction codes for LD HL, 63 D and LD BC, 45 D, using Appendix 2 are determined from

Operation:	$dd \leftarrow nn$
Op Code:	LD
Operands:	dd, nn

0	0	d	d	0	0	0	1
←			n				→
←			n				→

Description: The 2-byte integer nn is loaded to the dd register pair, where dd defines the BC, DE, HL, or SP register pairs, assembled as follows in the object code:

Pair	dd
BC	00
DE	01
HL	10
SP	11

The first n operand after the Op Code is the low order byte.

The operand required is a two-byte number consisting of a high byte 8 binary digits long and a low byte of the same length, in terms of which 63 D is therefore 0011 1111 (low byte) and 0000 0000 (high byte). Similarly, 45 D is 0010 1101 (low byte) 0000 0000 (high byte).

DETERMING THE BINARY OPERATION CODES FOR THE ASM MNEMONICS

Consider again he ASM instructions for

LD HL, 63 D

LD BC, 45 D

Referring to the previous page, the op. code for LD HL is determined from

0	0	d	d	0	0	0	1

where dd for HL is 10. This gives 0011 0001. Similarly, the op. code for LD BC is determined using dd = 00, giving 0000 0011.

THE BINARY CODE FOR THE COMPLETE INSTRUCTION

In the case of each of LD HL, 63 D and LD BC, 45 D we therefore have one byte of code for the operation and two bytes for the operand (the first being the low byte, the second the high byte of the binary equivalent of 63 D or 45 D). Each complete instruction in machine code therefore consists of 3 bytes, remembering that the low byte for each operands precedes the high byte:

LD HL, 65 D   0011 0001, 0011 1111, 0000 0000

LD BC, 45 D   0000 0011, 0010 1101, 0000 0000

To go on to add the two numbers, the ASM instruction

ADD HL,BC

can be used. This has no operands, which have already been loaded into the HL and BC register pairs using the previous two instructions

LD HL, 65 D

LD BC, 45 D

The machine code instruction for ADD HL,BC using Appendix 1 is determined from

ADD HL, ss

Operation:	$HL \leftarrow HL + ss$
Op Code:	ADD
Operands:	HL, ss

0	0	s	s	1	0	0	1

Description: The contents of register pair ss (any of register pairs BC, DE, HL, or SP) are added to the contents of register pair HL and the result is stored in HL. Operand ss is specified as follows in the assembled object code.

Register Pair	ss
BC	00
DE	01
HL	10
SP	11

Since ss is DE in this case, ss = 01 and the required binary code for the operation is therefore 0001 1001. The complete instruction in machine code therefore consists of 1 byte:

ADD HL,BC   0001 1001

The other ASM instructions used in the programs in the previous chapter can be coded in binary in a similar way, each requiring 1-3 bytes.

ASSIGNING MEMORY ADDRESSES TO EACH INSTRUCTION

In order to execute a machine code program, a memory address must assigned to each instruction. It was explained earlier that execution of the program is controlled by the program counter which always contains the address of the next instruction to be executed. For example, suppose for simplicity of explanation the memory address of the first instruction to be executed is 32768 D, which is 2^{15} and is a two-byte number equal to 1000 0000 0000 0000B. Returning to the ASM program consisting of the three instructions:

LD HL, 63 D
LD BC, 45 D
ADD HL,BC

the binary code for the instructions was determined to be:

LD HL, 65 D   0011 0001, 0011 1111, 0000 0000

LD BC, 45 D   0000 0011, 0010 1101, 0000 0000

ADD HL,BC   0001 1001

The first instruction to be executed is LD HL, 65 D which is allocated the memory address of 32 768 D. The op. code together with the two operands take up three bytes of memory, and so the next instruction to be executed, LD BC, 45 D is allocated the address 32 768 + 3 D = 32 771 D. LD BC, 45 D also requires 3 bytes of memory, and so memory address 32 771 + 3 D = 32 774 D is assigned to ADD HL,BC. In the machine code program containing these three instructions, all values must be in binary, and so the denary addresses must also be converted into their binary equivalents.

The total binary code for any program of reasonable length, for example Example 5 in Ch. 4 would therefore be quite extensive, and installing this code in memory directly would be a tedious and error-prone procedure. However, the binary code can first be converted into *hexadecimal* and installed from *BASIC* running on the *Z80* based *380Z* microcomputer. This is described in the next chapter.

6. INSTALLING AND EXECUTING THE PROGRAM FROM *BASIC*

CONVERTING THE BINARY CODE INTO HEXADECIMAL

The binary codes may be converted into hexadecimal using Appendix 3 , and will be illustrated using the Example 1 program in Ch. 4. The entire binary code for this program was found to be:

0010 0001,0011 1111,0000 0000,0000 0001,0010 1101,0000 0000,0000 1001

The starting address for the program was 1000 0000 0000 0000 (32 768 D) and the last address 1000 0000 0000 0110 (32 774 D).

Using Appendix 3, these binary codes in hexadecimal are:

Instruction codes 21 H, 3F H, 00 H, 2D H, 00 H, 09 H

Memory address (1st and last instructions): 8000 H, 8005 H

INSTALLING THE HEXADECIMAL CODES IN MEMORY

POKE INSTRUCTIONS

The instruction in *BASIC* which is used to install a data byte into memory is POKE. In *BASIC* hexadecimal numbers are prefixed by an ampersand &. For example, 21 H is represented as &21. The POKE instruction has two arguments, the first is an address up to two bytes long, and the second is the data byte to be stored at that address. For example, to store the data byte &21 at memory address &8000, the instruction POKE &8000,&21 would be used. However, since a block of consecutive memory addresses is normally used for programs, addresses for the POKE instructions may be supplied using a DATA file. This is explained in the next sub-section.

DATA FILES

A data file consists of a list of data bytes separated by commas, following the word DATA. For the hexadecimal codes of the Example 1 program this would be:

DATA &21, &3F, &00, &2D, &00, &09

Each data value can be inputted by a READ instruction. This procedure is facilitated by making READ a part of a FOR-NEXT loop to input each data value in the DATA list consecutively. FOR-NEXT loops are considered next.

FOR-NEXT LOOPS

Consider the following *BASIC* statements:

FOR P=1 TO 6
POKE P,Q
NEXT P

The value of P is the memory address at which the data value Q is stored, choosing simple numbers for P for the purposes of explanation. This FOR-NEXT loop has the same effect as:

POKE 1,Q
POKE 2,Q
POKE 3,Q

```
POKE 4,Q
POKE 5,Q
POKE 6,Q
```

This gives consecutive addresses for the POKEs as required, but the same data value is stored at each of the 6 memory address, whereas consecutive memory addresses storing different data values are required, i.e.:

```
POKE 1,Q₁
POKE 2,Q₂
POKE 3,Q₃
POKE 4,Q₄
POKE 5,Q₅
POKE 6,Q₆
```

Where Q_1 to Q_6 may all be different.
This can be achieved by READing the Q_1 to Q_6 from a DATA list as follows:

```
FOR P=1 TO 6
READ Q
POKE P,Q
NEXT P
```

If the range of P is changed to &8000 TO &8005, and the Q_1 to Q_6 in the DATA list are the hexadecimal codes for the Example 1 program, the following *BASIC* statements:

FOR P=&8000 TO &8005
READ Q
POKE P,Q
NEXT Q
DATA &21,&3F,&00,&2D,&00,&09
will have the same effect as:

POKE &8000,&21
POKE &8001,&3F
POKE &8002,&00
POKE &8003,&2D
POKE &8004,&00
POKE &8005,&09

as required.

ESSENTIAL 'BOOK-KEEPING' ASPECTS OF BASIC NEEDED

NUMBERING LINES OF STATEMENTS IN BASIC

In *BASIC* each statement or *line* must be given a number, and each line is executed in turn. Standard practice is to number the first line 10 and subsequent statements 20, 30, 40, etc.

CLEARING MEMORY FOR THE MACHINE CODE PROGRAM

This is done with the CLEAR instruction, two arguments, one setting the stack memory space and the other the space for the instructions of the machine code program. The values used for the arguments are not critical as long as they are ample.

PREVENTING THE MEMORY AREA USED FOR THE MACHINE CODE PROGRAM BEING OVERWRITTEN

This is achieved by POKE-ing two particular addresses in memory with the low byte and high byte of the starting address of the program, as will be shown shortly.

EXECUTING THE MACHINE CODE PROGRAM

This is accomplished when the *BASIC* programme is executed using the instruction CALL, whose argument is the start address of the program.

RETURNING TO BASIC AFTER EXECUTING THE MACHINE CODE PROGRAM

At the end of the machine code program, an instruction must be included which returns control to basic. The mnemonic for this is RET and its operand is the return address to BASIC. This address is put on the stack by *BASIC* when the machine code program is CALL-ed. From Appendix 1, the binary code for RET is 1100 1001 which is C9 H.

EXECUTING THE BASIC PROGRAM

The completed *BASIC* program is executed using the CP/M control word loadgo.

THE COMPLETE BASIC PROGRAM TO INSTALL IN MEMORY AND EXECUTE THE MACHINE CODE PROGRAM PERFORMING SIMPLE ADDITION OF TWO NUMBERS

Adding in all the necessary book-keeping functions, the complete *BASIC* program to install and execute the Example 1 program on the *380 Z* is:

```
10 CLEAR 100,,500
20 POKE 711C,&FF
30 POKE &11D,&7F
40 FOR P=&8000 to &8005
50 READ Q
60 POKE P,Q
70 NEXT Q
80 DATA &21,&3F,&00,&2D,&00,&09,&C9
90 CALL &8000
loadgo
```

7. DEVELOPING THE GRAPHICS MACHINE CODE PROGRAM

This chapter describes the stages of development of the circle and arc plotting machine code program, beginning with a program to plot a single 'pixel' or graphics dot, moving on to a program to plot all the dots necessary to display a full circle and finally the full program which plots a circle or part of a circle with centre co-ordinates defined by the user. The full machine code program is CALL-ed from *BASIC* using the instruction "CIRCLE" which has 5 arguments. These are the start and finish points of the circle arc to be plotted, the X and Y centre co-ordinates and finally the intensity. The program uses the machine code subroutine "PLOT" which is a part of the basicsg2 graphics facility used on the *380 Z*. This will be described next.

THE "PLOT" SUBROUTINE IN *BASIC*

This plots a single graphics dot when CALL-ed from *BASIC*. It has 3 arguments, 2 for the X and Y screen co-ordinates of the dot and 1 for the intensity of the dot to be displayed. As discussed previously, the problem in CALL-ing this subroutine from *BASIC* is that execution of the instruction is too slow for plotting the 300-odd dots of a circle 50 screen positions diameter required in the *BASIC* graphics teaching program.

A MACHINE CODE PROGRAM TO PLOT A SINGLE GRAPHICS POINT

An ASM program to plot a point at X, Y=176 D with intensity 3 (white) is shown on the next page. Since the previous chapter has explained ASM programming in some detail it should be possible to follow the logic of the program as outlined in the comments following the semi-colons in each program statement.

	;return address to BASIC is put on stack when the ;machine code program is CALL-ed from BASIC
LD HL,&B0,&00	;X co-ord of point
PUSH HL	;Put X co-ord on stack
LD HL,&B0,&00	;Y co-ord of point
PUSH HL	;Put Y co-ord on stack
LD HL, &03,&00	;3 arguments for "PLOT"
PUSH HL	;put no. of arguments=3 on stack
JP &B8,&35	;the address of "PLOT" subroutine in BASIC
POP HL	;3 arguments
POP BC	;Y co-ord
POP DE	;X co-ord
	;return address to BASIC is now on top of stack
RET	;return to BASIC

ASSEMBLY LANGUAGE PROGRAM TO PLOT A SINGLE GRAPHICS POINT

The machine codes in hexadecimal for the program are in lines 40 and 50 of the original print-out of the *BASIC* program shown below, which is used to install and execute it. The functions of the statements in the other lines of the *BASIC* program are the same as the corresponding statements previously discussed for the simple addition addition machine code program. Note that several statements may be used in the same line by separating statements with colons.

BASIC program to install and execute the machine code single graphics point- plotting program

```
***THIS PROGRAM PUTS X,Y COORDS AND INTENSITY OF 1 POINT ON THE STACK
JPS TO <PLOT> SUBROUTINE IN BASICSG2 INTERPRETER,AND PLOTS THE POINT IN HIGH RES***

**THE X,Y ARE &B0,&B0=176,176.THE INTENSITY IS 3**

*THE X,Y,AND N ARE POP'ED OFF THE STACK PRIOR TO RETURN MACH LANG PROG TO BASIC*


10 CLEAR 100,,500
15 CALL"RESOLUTION",0,2
20 POKE&11C,&6C:POKE&11D,&7A
30 FORP=&7A80TO&7A94:READQ:POKEP,Q:NEXTP
40 DATA&21,&B0,&00,&E5,&21,&B0,&00,&E5,&21,&03,&00,&E5
50 DATA&0E,&03,&C3,&BB,&35,&E1,&C1,&D1,&C9
60 CALL&7A80
90 PRINT"DONE"
```

EXTENDING THE PROGRAM TO PLOT A FULL CIRCLE
PLOTTING THE CIRCLE POINTS IN BASIC

In order to plot a circle in *BASIC*, the program shown on the next page was tried. Referring to that listing and the diagram on p. 78 , line 10 generates the X-Y co-ordinates of the first quadrant of points to plot, using sine and cosine functions, scaled for a circle of radius 50, with 128 points per quadrant. Line 20 then generates the co-ordinates of the points in the remaining three quadrants by mathematical reflection in the x and y axes, at the time translating them for a circle centre of co-ordinates 50,50. As each pair of co-ordinates is calculated, the X and Y are passed to the "PLOT" subroutine for display as discussed previously. This is carried out in line 40. A FOR-NEXT loop, which were also explained previously, enables 4 points to be plotted (1 in each quadrant) for each calculated X and Y 128 times. This gives 4 x 128 =512 points to plot and 1024 X,Y co-ordinates.

```
10 FOR I=1 TO 128:J=COS(I/82)*50:K=SIN(I/82)*50

20 J1=J+50:J2=-J1:K1=K+50:K2=-K1

30 CALL "PLOT",J1,K1,3:CALL "PLOT",J2,K1,3:CALL "PLOT",J1,K2,3:CALL
"PLOT",J2,K2,3

40 NEXT I
```

Program in BASIC to plot a Graphics Circle

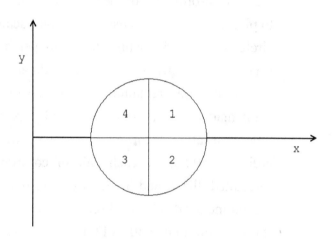

The four Quadrants of Circle Points

CREATING A DATA FILE FOR THE CO-ORDINATES OF THE CIRCLE POINTS

As noted previously, this 'dot-by-dot' calculation and plot method of producing a graphics circle in *BASIC* took too long. It was therefore decided to use the same method of calculating the co-ordinates of the points, but then instead of PLOT-ing them immediately in *BASIC* to save them in a DATA file. Data files were explained previously. These could then be installed in memory using POKE statements. Without calculating the co-ordinates each time, these could be fetched from memory by a machine code program and plotted.

A copy of the original print-out of the data file, "DATA"is shown on the next page.

```
10 CREATE£10,"DATA"
20 FORI=1TO128:J=COS(I/82)*50:K=SIN(I/82)*50
30 Q=INT(J+50.5)
40 PRINT£10,Q:PRINTQ
50 Q=INT(K+50.5)
60 PRINT£10,Q:PRINTQ
70 Q=INT(50.5-K)
80 PRINT£10,Q:PRINTQ
90 Q=INT(50.5-J)
100 PRINT£10,Q:PRINTQ
110 NEXTI
120 CLOSE£10
```

DATA file which Calculates then stores the 1024 Co-ordinates
of points of a Circle Radius 50, Centre (50,50)

CREATING THE POKES PROGRAM IN BASIC TO INSTALL THE CO-ORDINATES OF THE CIRCLE POINTS IN MEMORY

A block of 1024 bytes (400 H) of memory, starting at address &68E0 was used to store the co-ordinates of the circle points. A copy of the original program in *BASIC* used to do this is shown on the next page. Referring to that print-out, after opening the file "DATA" in line 10, each INPUT instruction fetches one data item from the file in the variable Q. Corresponding to the four circle quadrants as explained above, each data item, x or y, is stored in memory by the lines 50, 70, 90 and 110 in memory locations such that &68E0 contains the x co-ordinate of the first point, &68E1 the y co-ordinate of the first point; &68E2 and &68E3 the x and y co-ordinates of the second point, and so on until all the 512 pairs of x-y co-ordinates have been stored in successive memory locations. After the last data item has been input from the file, it is closed by line 20. Control is then passed to line 130 which loads the machine code program to plot the circle, which will now be described.

```
Ready:
LOAD"POKES"

Ready:
LIST

5 POKE&11C,&9F:POKE&11D,&67
7 CLEAR1,,1400
10 OPEN£10,"DATA"
20 ONEOFGOTO130
30 A=&68E0:B=&68E1:C=&68E0+&100:D=&68E1+&100:E=&68E0+&200:F=&68E1+&200:G=&68E0+&
40 INPUT£10,Q
50 POKEA,Q:POKED,Q:A=A+2:D=D+2
60 INPUT£10,Q
70 POKEB,Q:POKE8,Q:B=B+2:G=G+2
80 INPUT£10,Q
90 POKEC,Q:POKEF,Q:C=C+2:F=F+2
100 INPUT£10,Q
110 POKEE,Q:POKEH,Q:E=E+2:H=H+2
120 GOTO40
130 LOAD&GO"CIRCLE"
```

Program in BASIC which stores the co-ordinates of the points of a Circle from a
DATA file in Memory

THE FULL CIRCLE PLOTTING MACHINE CODE PROGRAM

A copy of the original ASM program is shown on the next two pages, which also shows the op. codes, converted to hexadecimal, in the right hand column. The purpose of the instruction in each ASM statement is explained in the comment fields, but some additional explanation is in order.

CALLing the machine code program from *BASIC* automatically places the return address to *BASIC* in the stack. The instructions in the opening ASM statements POP this off the stack and temporarily store it in memory. The address of the x co-ordinate of the first point is loaded into HL and ComPared with the address of the x co-ordinate of the final point. If they are the same, the y co-ordinate is checked similarly. If they are the same, the program RETurns control to *BASIC*. If they are not the same, the address of the x and y of the point are stored in memory, the point is plotted, and HL is incremented to the address of the x co-ordinate of the next point. The x co-ordinate of this point is then ComPared with the previous point, in the address retrieved from memory. If these are the same, the y co-ordinates are compared. If these are also the same, the present point and the previous point are the same, the point is not plotted (because it has already been plotted) and HL is incremented twice to point to the address of the next point. This results in a significant improvement in the speed with which the circle is plotted, as the following discussion shows.

A simple program in *BASIC* was written to calculate the integer values x and y co-ordinates of the circle points of the first quadrant, shown on page 78. The results are tabulated on page 87.

Z80 ASM Program to Plot a full Circle

;QUICKPLOT ASSEMBLY LANGUAGE PROG.

		Op.Cod
POP HL	;unstack RETURN addr. to BASIC	&E1
LD(&7B08),HL	;store it	&22
LD HL,00,00		&21
EXX	;use aux. regs.	&D9
LD HL,&6537	;starting addr. for x,y of points	&21
LD A,H =NEXT		&7C
CP 69	;compare high byte of addr. for last x,y of points with present addr	&FE
JP NZ,CONT1		&C2
LD A,L		&7D
CP 3A	;repeat with low byte	&FE
JP Z,DONE	;if last x,y,RETURN to BASIC	&CA
LD A,(HL) =CONT1	;put x of point in Accumulator	&7E
EXX	;use main regs.	&D9
LD HL,&7B08	;load addr. of x of last point	&21
CP (HL)	;compare with present x of point	&BE
JP NZ,CONT2	;if not same,plot point	&C2
EXX	;use aux regs	&D9
INC HL	;addr of y of point	&23
LD A,(HL)	;y in Accumulator	&7E
EXX	;main regs	&D9
LD HL,&7B07	;load Addr. of y of last point	&21
CP (HL)	;compare with y of present point	&BE
JP Z,MISS	;if same as last point,don't PLOTit	&CA
EXX	;aux regs	&D9
DEC HL	;addr of x in HL ready for PLOT	&2B
EXX	;main regs	&D9
EXX =CONT2	;aux regs	&D9
LD A,HL	;start of plotting sequence	&7E
EXX	;main regs	&D9
LD BC,00,00		&01
LD C,A	;x of point into BC	&4F
EXX	;aux regs	&D9
INC HL	;addr of y of point	&23
LD A,HL	;y of point into accumulator	&7E
EXX	;main regs	&D9
LD DE,00,00		&11
LD E,A	;y of point into DE	&5F
LD HL,&7ACC	;RET addr. from PLOT in BASICSU2 interpreter	&21
PUSH HL	;stackit	&E5
PUSH BC	;stack x	&C5
PUSH DE	;stack y	&D5

```
LD C,&03          ;3 arguments for PLOT                        &0B
LD DE,&00,&03     ;intensity of points                        &11
PUSH DE           ;stack it                                    &D5
JP &35BB          ;addr. of FLOT in BASICSG2                   &C3
                   interpreter
EXX               ;aux regs                                    &D9
LD A,(HL)                                                      &7E
EXX               ;main regs                                   &D9
LD(7307),A        ;load y of point,store it for               &32
                   comparison with next point
EXX               ;aux regs                                    &D9
DEC HL                                                         &2B
LD A,(HL)         ;                                            &7E
EXX               ;main regs                                   &D9
LD(&7B06),A       ;store x of point for comparison            &32
EXX               ;aux regs                                    &D9
INC HL                                                         &23
INC HL            ;addr of x of next point                    &23
JP NEXT           ;process NEXT point                          &C3
EXX  =DONE        ;finished PLOTting CIRCLE                    &D9
                   main regs
LD HL,(&7B08)     ;load addr of RETURN to BASIC               &2A
PUSH HL           ;stack it                                    &E5
RET               ;RETURN to BASIC                             &C9
EXX  =MISS        ;aux regs                                    &D9
INC HL            ;addr of x of next point                    &23
JP NEXT                                                        &C3
```

Z80 ASM PROGRAM TO DRAW A FULL CIRCLE

10 FOR I=1 TO 128:PRINT INT((COS(I/82)*50.5),PRINT INT(50-(SIN(I/82)*50.5)

20 NEXT I

Program in BASIC used to calculate the integer values of
the x and y co-ordinates of the 128 graphics points of the
first quadrant of the circle

Table containing the integer values of the x, y co-ordinates of the 128 points of the first quadrant of the circle.

* indicates that the co-ordinates of the point are repeated.

X	Y	R	X	Y	R	X	Y	R	X	Y	R	X	Y	R
100	49		100	49	*	100	48		100	48	*	100	47	
100	46		100	48	*	100	45		100	45	*	100	44	
100	43		99	43		99	42		99	42	*	99	41	
99	40		99	40	*	99	39		99	39	*	99	38	
98	37		98	37	*	98	36		98	36	*	98	35	
98	34		97	34		97	33		97	33	*	97	32	
96	32		96	31		96	30		96	30	*	96	29	
95	29		95	28		95	28	*	94	27		94	27	*
94	26		94	25		93	25		93	24		93	24	*
92	23		92	23	*	92	22		91	22		91	21	
91	21	*	90	20		90	20	*	90	19		89	19	
89	18		88	18		88	18	*	88	17		87	17	
87	16		86	16		86	15		86	15	*	85	14	
85	14	*	84	14		84	13		83	13		83	12	
82	12		82	12	*	81	11		81	11	*	81	10	

X	Y	R	X	Y	R	X	Y	R	X	Y	R	X	Y	R
80	10		81	10	*	79	9		79	9	*	78	9	
78	8		77	8		77	8	*	76	7		75	7	
75	7	*	74	6		74	6	*	73	6		73	5	
72	5		72	5	*	71	5		71	4		70	4	
69	4		69	4	*	68	3		68	3	*	67	3	
67	3	*	66	3		65	2		65	2	*	64	2	
64	2	*	63	2		63	2	*	62	1		61	1	
61	1	*	60	1		60	1	*	59	1		58	1	
58	1	*	57	1		57	0		56	0		55	0	
55	0	*	54	0		54	0	*	53	0		52	0	
52	0	*	51	0		50	0							

Note that 40 points out of the 128 are repeated-almost one-third. The same number, of course occurs with the other three quadrants. So the circle is plotted just as well using 4 x (128-40) = 352 points stored in 704 memory addresses as 4x128 = 512 points stored in 1024 addresses. Hence, since the additional instructions required to test whether successive points have the same co-ordinates take far less time to execute than a call to PLOT to plot the point unnecessarily, a significant improvement in speed results. This is important because as explained previously, the circle has to be plotted in the *BASIC* teaching program in white and then in black successively to create the illusion of movement around the screen, which must take place at a reasonable speed.

The remaining features of the ASM program are adequately explained in the comment field and the use of the stack is the same as that already described for the previous program which plots a single point. The same remarks apply to the *BASIC* program used to install and execute the program after conversion into binary and then hexadecimal as described previously.

ADDING USER FEATURES TO THE FULL CIRCLE PLOTTING MACHINE CODE PROGRAM

The previous program could only plot a full circle in white with fixed centre at 50,50. So that any desired part of a circle (radius 50) could be plotted in white or black anywhere on the screen, arguments for the start and finish points of the part of the circle required, arguments for the co-ordinates of the circle centre and an argument for the colour had to be incorporated into the program.

To enable the user to pass the appropriate arguments to the program, a "CALL" in BASIC with the 5 arguments described above needed to be included in the program instructions. The way this was done will be described shortly. When the program is called, *BASIC* automatically stores the arguments in the stack. In the first part of the ASM program shown on p. 93, these are successively POPed off the stack and loaded into the HL pair of registers and then stored in memory. The first two arguments, S and F set the addresses in which the co-ordinates of the points are stored at which plotting is to start and finish, giving the orientation and length of arc required by the user. The value of S is added to the absolute starting address of the block of memory where the 1024 coordinates of the circle points are stored. The value of F is used to determine the address of the co-ordinates of the finishing point, instead of using the address of the final point of the complete circle (absolute starting address + 1023 and 1024 D) in the previous program.

With the next two arguments the user determines the centre co-ordinates of the circle or part circle (arc). These are added to each co-ordinate of each point prior to plotting.

The final argument is for colour in the range 1 to 3 which is accessed by the PLOT subroutine as will be explained shortly.

With the 5 arguments stored in memory, S is loaded into HL; the absolute starting address of the block of memory where the 1024 circle co-ordinates are stored is loaded into DE and these two values are added in HL to give the starting address for the x co-ordinate of first point of the arc. This is repeated for the y co-ordinate. After PLOTing the point, HL, containing the address of the point just plotted is incremented twice to process the next point, as described for the previous program, for both x and y co- ordinates. Each is then compared with their (consecutive) finish addresses as calculated above. If they are the same, the arc is finished and control is passed back to *BASIC* via a RETurn instruction as described in the previous program. The bottom third of the program on p. 93 adds the user determined x and y co-ordinates of the centre of the circle to the appropriate x and y values in the addresses of the points for the full circle stored in the 1024 bytes of memory, and these are then passed to the PLOT subroutine in *BASIC*. The main purpose of at this stage of program development was to successfully produce a program which incorporated the five arguments, without complicating the program by including instructions to appropriately transform the arguments. These could be added in at the final stage of program development.

Z80 program to draw a circle and arcs with user-defined centre,
start & finishing points and intensity

```
                              ;Z80 Assembly Language Program to quickPLOT
                              ; Circles,Sectors,Quadrants and Slices
                              ;BASIC entry code is CALL "CIRCLE",start,
                              ;finish,x-centre,y-centre,intensity (*S,F,X,
                              ;Y,N)
        POP  HL               ;unstack and store S,F,X,Y,N
        LD (&7D10),HL         ;(N) intensity
        POP  HL
        LD (&7D12),HL         ;Y coord of centre
        POP  HL
        LD (&7D14),HL         ;X coord of centre
        POP  HL
        LD (&7D16),HL         ;(F) finishing point of Arc
        POP  HL
        LD (&7D18),HL         ;(S) starting point of Arc
        LD HL,&7A80           ;absolute start address for points
        LD DE,(&7D18)
        ADD HL,DE             ;start address for points
        RES 0,L               ;1st address for points must be "x"(not "y")
        LD DE,0
        EX DE,HL
        LD BC,(&7D16)         ;finish point of Arc
        LD HL,(&7A80)
        ADD HL,BC             ;HL contains start address for points
        EX DE,HL              ;DE contains finish address  "
        RES 0,E               ;finish address for points must be "x"
NEXT:   LD A,H                ;load high byte of address of point
        CP &7D                ;
        JP Z,DONE             ;full circle PLOTted,RETurn to BASIC
        LD A,D                ;load high byte of finish address
        CP H                  ;
        JP NZ,CONT            ;if not DONE PLOTting,CONTinue
        LD A,E
        CP L
        JP Z,DONE             ;No more points to PLOT,Return to BASIC
CONT:   LD A,(&7D14)          ;Xlate x of point (x+Xcoord of centre)
        ADD A,(HL)            ;
        LD (HL),A
        LD C,A                ;Xlated x of point in BC
        LD B,&0
        INC HL                ;te y of point
        LD A,(&7D12)          ;
        ADD A,(HL)            ;Xlate y of point
```

```
        LD D,&0
        LD (HL),A
        LD E,A                ;Xlated y of point in DE
PLOT:   PUSH BC               ;stack x and y
        PUSH DE
        LD HL,(&7D10)         ;N
        LD C,&03              ;3 args for PLOT
        PUSH HL
        JP &35B8              ;to PLOT in BASICSG2 interpreter
        POP HL
        POP BC                ;RET address to stack top
        POP DE
        INC HL                ;pointer to address of next point
        JP,NEXT               ;process NEXT point

DONE:   RET
```

Z80 Program to draw a circle and arcs with user-defined
centre, start & finish points and intensity

Coming on to the method of "CALL"ing, with the 5 arguments, from *BASIC*, the method outlined to do this shown below. The addresses involved are 'book-keeping' features of the 380Z microcomputer

1. POKE the name of the program into the memory locations starting at (e.g.) address 7A70 H

2. POKE 2D61 H with the low byte of the start address of the program ie 70 H

3. POKE 2D62 H with the high byte of the start address of the program ie 7A H

4. The first three bytes of the program must be 00,00,(number of characters in the name of the program). The program was named 'circle' which has 6 characters, and so the first 3 bytes of the program are 00,00,06 H

5. Next follow the ASCII codes in hex for each character

6. Finally, the address of the start of program instructions is included. If this is 7A80 H, this gives:

00,00,06,43,49,52,43,4C,45,80,7A

```
The Procedure for setting up the "CALL" instruction and
arguments from BASIC
```

The machine code program is therefore executed from *BASIC* with the instruction
Call "Circle" S,F,X,Y,N.

The final part of the program places the arguments on the stack for the "PLOT" subroutine in *BASIC*.

THE FINAL STAGE OF DEVELOPMENT OF THE PROGRAM

A further improvement in speed might have been obtained by POKEing the 704 non-repeated co-ordinates of the points into memory, instead of the full set of 1024. Then, the extra program instructions to deal with repeated points could have been omitted, thereby speeding up program execution. But in practice, the speed with which the program drew full circles was found to be satisfactory for the intended use of the program, without this refinement.

In the previous program, the start S and finish F argument values were processed by the program without transformation. However, recalling that the starting address of the points was determined by adding S to the absolute starting address of the 1024 bytes of memory containing the x and y co-ordinates of the points, it is apparent that an argument for S in range 0 - 128 D will only enable arcs to be drawn starting up to 128/1024 = 1/8 from the starting point of the circle. A similar argument range for F will also only allow arcs to be plotted up to 1/8 of a full circle. A subroutine (loop) of extra instructions to multiply S and F by 8 prior to further processing by the program was therefore written. This is shown below. The operation SLA is illustrated below and the working of the loop is explained for the example S=85 D on p. 97.

```
                    x8 loop for S and F


                                        ;at entry S is in HL, H=0 so L=S

              LD B,0                     ;set B=0

              LD A,0                     ;set A=0

              LD D,3                     ;set D=3 (loop counter)

     SHIFT:   SLA L                      ;shift contents of L

              ADC B                      ;add carry flag to A

              DEC D                      ;decrement counter

              JPZ,END          ;if D=0, exit loop

              SLA A                      ;shift countents of A

              JP SHIFT

     END:     LD H,A                     ;HL=8xS
```

THE SLA (Shift Left Arithmetic)

Register contents (bits) are shifted one place to the left, with 0 going into the bit 0 position and bit 7 into the Carry Flag

The working of the x8 loop for the example argument S=85 D

0101 0101 B = 85D

1st time round loop

Register	Carry Flag	Register Contents	Instruction
D	0	0000 0011	LD D,3
L	0	1010 1010	SLA L
A	0	0000 0000	ADC B
D	0	0000 0010	DEC D
A	0	0000 0000	SLA A

2nd time round loop

L	1	0101 0100	SLA L
A	1	0000 0001	ADC B
D	1	0000 0001	DEC D
A	0	0000 0010	SLA A

3rd and final time round loop

L	0	1010 1000	SLA L
A	0	0000 0010	ADC B
D	0	0000 0000	DEC D

			END
HL		0000 0010 1010 1000	LD H,L

0000 0010 1010 1000 B = 680 D = 8x85 D

F can be multiplied by 8 similarly with the value of F in auxiliary register pair HL' and executing the instructions in the loop a second time after switching to aux registers using EXX.

A copy of the original print out of the completed machine code program in hexadecimal is shown below:

The BASIC program to install and execute the final circle machine code program

```
      LOAD"CIRCLE"

      Ready:
      LIST

17 POKE&33D9,&C0:POKE&33DA,&67
50 POKE&6CE0,&00:POKE&6CE1,&32:POKE&6CE2,&64:POKE&6CE3,&32
60 FORP=&67D0TO&68AA::READD:POKEP,D:NEXTP
70 DATA&E1,&22,&B0,&68,&E1,&22,&68,&E2,&68,&E1,&22,&B4,&68,&E1
72 DATA&22,&B6,&68,&E1,&22,&B8,&68,&E1,&22,&BA,&68,&D9,&21
74 DATA&E0,&68,&56,&00,&ED,&5B,&B8,&68,&3E,&08,&19,&30,&C2,&F4
76 DATA&67,&22,&BC,&68,&06,&00,&ED,&4B,&B6,&68,&21,&E0,&68
78 DATA&3E,&08,&09,&3D,&C2,&07,&68,&54,&5D,&2A,&BC,&68,&06,&00
79 DATA&7C,&BA
80 DATA&C2,&10,&68,&7D,&BB,&CA,&9C,&68,&7E,&32,&BE,&68,&D9,&3A
82 DATA&BE,&68,&21,&C0,&68,&BE,&C2,&A7,&68,&D9,&23,&7E,&32,&BE
84 DATA&68,&D9,&3A,&BE,&68,&21,&C2,&68,&BE,&CA,&A2,&68,&D9,&2B
86 DATA&7E,&32,&BE,&68,&D9,&3A,&BE,&68,&01,&32,&00,&26,&00,&6F
87 DATA&22,&C0,&68,&37,&3F,&ED,&42,&ED,&4B,&B4,&68,&09
88 DATA&06,&00,&44
90 DATA&4D,&D9,&23,&7E,&32,&BE,&68,&D9,&3A,&BE,&68
92 DATA&11,&32,&00,&26,&00,&6F,&22,&C2,&68,&37,&3F,&ED,&52,&ED
93 DATA&5B,&B2,&68,&19
94 DATA&22,&BE,&68,&ED,&5B,&BE,&68,&21,&92,&68,&E5,&C5,&D5,&0E
96 DATA&03,&56,&00,&ED,&5B,&B0,&68,&D5,&C3,&88,&35,&D9,&04,&78
97 DATA&32,&C4,&68
98 DATA&23,&C3,&13,&68,&D9,&2A,&BA,&68,&E5,&C9,&D9,&23
100 DATA&C3,&13,&68,&D9,&C3,&3F,&68
130 FORP=&67C0TO&67CA:READD:POKEP,D:NEXTP
140 DATA0,0,&06,&43,&49,&52,&43,&4C,&45,&D0,&67
```

8. USING THE PROGRAM TO GENERATE 'MOVING' GRAPHICS SHAPES

DRAWING CIRCLE SECTORS

The Circle program was used to draw fractional parts of circles as part of a *BASIC* graphics teaching program. In addition to the whole 1, the fractional parts involved were 1/2s, 1/4s, 1/3s and 1/10s, in various orientations at various screen positions. Referring back to p. 78 containing the *BASIC* program to generate the x-y co-ordinates of the circle points, it can be seen from the first line:

10 FOR I=1 to 128:J=COS(I/82)*50: K=SIN(I/82)*50

that when I=1 (first point) J=50 and K=0, and when I=128 J=0 and K=50

Now the bottom, left-hand corner of the 380Z graphics screen is (0,0), so the first quadrant of the circle is plotted upwards and anti-clockwise. The x and y of the points are translated by 50.5, so for example, the instruction Call "Circle" 0,32,x,y,n (with suitable values for x,y and n) will produce a 1/4 of a circle starting at its rightmost position and plotted upwards towards the left. 32/128=1/4. To display an arc of length 1/2, S is set to 128/2=64; for 1/3 of the circle, S is set 128/3=43; for 1/10 128/10=13 (nearest integer values: integer values only are displayed by the PLOT subroutine). The effects of various S and F arguments are illustrated below:

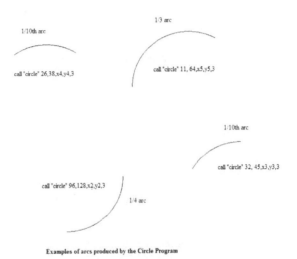

1/10th arc

call "circle" 26,38,x4,y4,3

1/3 arc

call "circle" 11, 64,x5,y5,3

1/10th arc

call "circle" 32, 45,x3,y3,3

call "circle" 96,128,x2,y2,3

1/4 arc

Examples of arcs produced by the Circle Program

USING THE "LINE" SUBROUTINE IN *BASIC* WITH "CIRCLE"

A straight line is drawn , using a PLOT instruction with arguments for the beginning of the line, followed by a LINE instruction for the end of the line. For example:

call "plot" 100,50,3:call "line" 150,50,3

draws a (horizontal) white line from (100,50) to (150,50).

Circle sectors can therefore be drawn by drawing an appropriate length arc using CIRCLE and drawing two lines, produced by a PLOT instruction for the start of the arc, then a LINE instruction to the centre, followed by another LINE instruction to the finish of the arc. For example,

call "circle" 0,32, 150,150,3
call "plot" 200,150,3
call "line" 150,150,3
call "line" 150,200,3

draws the 1/4 sector:

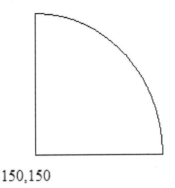

150,150

Some examples from the *BASIC* graphics teaching program will now be given, referring to copies of original printouts of sections of the program. The next page shows one such print-out. At lines 41000, 41100 and 41200 are *BASIC* routines which draw the three 1/3s of a circle (circle sectors) in three complementary directions. The values of centres x,y are variables can set by the main program. The effect of each these is shown on the page after.

Print-out of part of the BASIC graphics teaching program using "circle"

```
5300  GOSUB41500:IF=GET(397):IADHR9(E)<137*THEN6300
5310  N=0:GOSUB41500
5320  IFB<40THEN8=80
5329  M=3:GOSUB6200:GOSUB41600:IFB=5:GOTO5300
5360  GOSUB62001IFI=32THENGOSUB6300
5370  GOTO570
6000  A1=A:B1=B:ONRGOTO6070,6050,6040,6060
6010  RETURN
6020  GOSUB7010:GOSUB7020:GOSUB7020:GOTO6050
6030  GOSUB7000:GOSUB7020:GOSUB7030:GOTO6050
6040  GOSUB7000:GOSUB7010:GOSUB7050:GOTO6050
6050  A=A1:B=B1
6060  RETURN
6100  ONRGOTO6120,6130,6140,6150
6120  A=A1:B=B1:RETURN
6130  A=A2:B=B2:RETURN
6140  A=A2:B=BC:RETURN
6150  P=A21:9=B21:RETURN
6200  ONRGOTO6220,6230,6240,6250
6220  PA=A1BA=B:RETURN
6230  AB=A1BB=B:RETURN
6240  AC=A1BC=B:RETURN
6250  AD=A1BD=B:RETURN
6300  IFA>=150THENR=R+1:RETURN
6310  GOTO340
7000  A=A1:B=B1:GOSUB41000:RETURN
7010  A=AA:B=B1:GOSUB41500:RETURN
7020  A=AC1B=BC:GOSUB41500:RETURN
7030  A=AD:B=BD:GOSUB41500:RETURN
30400 CALL "CHARSIZE",N1,N:CALL "STPLOT",2,Y,VARADR(A),N:N=1:RETURN
40000 CALL"PLOT",A,B,N:CALL"LINE",C,B:CALL"LINE",C,D:CALL"LINE",A,D:CALL"LINE",A,B:RET
40100 CALL"CIRCLE",75,125,X,Y,N:CALL"PLOT",X+50,Y,N:CALL"LINE",X,Y:CALL"LINE",X,Y-50:R
40600 A2=A:B2=B:C2=C:D2=D:A=A1:B=7:ONA+70:DW0:GOSUB40000:CALL"PLOT",A,2,N:CALL"LINE",A
+75:N=1:GOSUB34700:A=A2:B=B2
40610 C=C2:D=D2:RETURN
40650 A=A*1*:GOSUB50400:GOSUB40050:RETURN
40860 CALL"PLOT",X,Y-7,N:CALL"LINE",Y+8,Y-3:RETURN
41000 CALL"CIRCLE",32,75,X,Y,N:CALL"PLOT",X+83,Y+25,N:CALL"LINE",3,Y:CALL"LINE",X,Y-50
41100 CALL"CIRCLE",117,125,X,Y,N:CALL"CIRCLES",6,32,X,Y,N:CALL"PLOT",X+43,Y-25,N:CALL"L
       INE",X,Y+50:RETURN
41200 CALL"CIRCLE",75,117,X,Y,N:CALL"PLOT",X-43,Y-25,N:CALL"LINE",X,Y:CALL"LINE",X+43,Y
       Y:
41300 C=A+50:D=B-50:GOSUB60000:A=*1*:B=*1*:C=*9*:X=A+22:Y=B-25:GOSUB40600:RETURN
41900 A=A+50:B=*9*:A=*0*:GOSUB60000:Y=Y+*17*:A=*8*:B=B*3:GOSUB30400:Y=V=17:RETURN
41800 C=A+100:B=B-25:GOSUB40000:A=*1*:B=*4*:Y=A+*47:Y=B+31:GOSUB41400:RETURN
41400 CALL"PLOT",150,140,N:CALL"LINE",150,20:CALL"LINE",215,25:CALL"LINE",215,190:CALL
       :190:RETURN
43000 GOSUB43400:A=A:B=1:C=1*0:C-R=13:GOSUB40000:A=A3+*10:B=B-30:C=A+1:D=1*2:GOSUB4900:B
       :GOSUB490:Q=A+1:C=A+13
43010 B=70:D=57:GOSUB40000:A=**:I=43+2:Y=80:GOSUB30400:A=**:I=A2+10:Y=4:GOSUB3040
       7*,63+10,44,N:CALL"LINE",63+20,14
43020 A=**)*:Y=63+15:Y=20:GOSUB30400:CALL"PLOT",A3+20,24:CALL"LINE",A5+10,24:CALL"PLOT
       ALL"LINE",A3+7,10
43500 CALL"PLOT",A3+5,5:CALL"LINE",A3-7,3:CALL"LINE",A3+9,5:RETURN
43600 D=A:A3+*2:B=*2:C=*A+25:GOSUB40000:CALL"PLOT",A,2,N:CALL"LINE",C,3:A6=*8*:X=A:Y=
       00:A6=**:X=A+5:GOSUB0400)
43610 A6=*1*:X=A+10:GOSUB34400:A6=*1*:Y=A+15:GOSUB30400:RETURN
49500 P1=B:D=100:FOR=1:T01:N=0:GOSUB30400:GOSUB50000:N=5:GOSUB30400:NEXT:R
       N
49500 CALL"PLOT",A,B,N:CALL"LINE",A+5,B-3:CALL"LINE",A+25,B-15:RETURN
49900 CALL"PLOT",A,B,N:CALL"LINE",A,B-7:CALL"LINE",A-3,B-4:CALL"PLOT",A,B-7:CALL"LINE",
       :RETURN
50000 FORP=3700:NEXT:F:RETURN
60000 GOSUB60600:I=GET(397):Z=BIT(C0:1:N=0:GOSUB30400:M=S:IFI=32THEN34060
```

The 1/3 sectors produced by three subroutines in the BASIC graphics teaching program

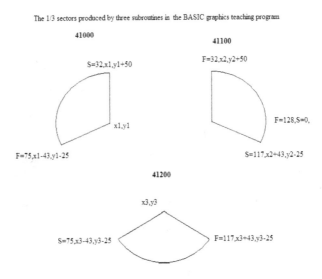

41000

S=32,x1,y1+50

x1,y1

F=75,x1-43,y1-25

41100

F=32,x2,y2+50

F=128,S=0,

S=117,x2+43,y2-25

41200

x3,y3

S=75,x3-43,y3-25

F=117,x3+43,y3-25

A more general sector-plotting subroutine can be written by using the values of the S and F parameters to determine the end points of the two straight sides to the sector. It will be remembered that a block of 1024 bytes (400 H) of memory, starting at address &68E0 was used to store the co-ordinates of the circle points. In the circle machine code program, S is multiplied by 8 and added to the absolute start address of the points &68E0 to give the user-determined starting address of the points. The x co-ordinate of this point is then added to the x co-ordinate of the centre, X, to give the x screen co-ordinate of the starting point of the arc. The absolute starting address for the y co-ordinate of the points is &68E1 and this is used in a similar way to give the y co-ordinate of the starting point of the arc. The co-ordinates of the last point of the arc are determined by multiplying F by 8, adding the result to &68E0 and &68E1, fetching untranslated the x,y values from the resulting addresses and translating them by adding X and Y.

So, the x,y arguments for the PLOT instruction for the straight lines of the sector are given by X,Y and the LINE arguments by (the contents of memory address &68E0+8S)+X, (the contents of memory address &68E1+8S)+Y; (the contents of memory address &68E0+8F)+X, (the contents of memory address &68E1+8F)+Y as shown below.

The *BASIC* instruction PEEK with a memory address argument fetches the contents at that memory address. A *BASIC* subroutine to plot any size sector anywhere on the graphics screen with any intensity starting at line 42200, for example, is shown on the following page.

Plotting a general circle sector

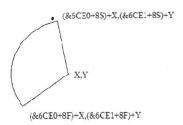

(&6CE0−8S) etc., refers to the contents of the memory address result in brackets

General sector-plotting subroutine in BASIC

```
42200 CALL "CIRCLE" S,F,X,Y,N
42210 CALL "PLOT" X,Y,N:CALL "LINE" PEEK(&68E0+8S)+X,PEEK(&68E1+8S)+Y,N
42220 CALL "PLOT" X,Y,N:CALL "LINE" PEEK(&68E0+8F)+X,PEEK(&68E1+8F)+Y,N
42230 RETURN
```

DRAWING CIRCLE 'SLICES'

The *BASIC* graphics teaching program aims to teach fraction concepts by not only providing examples of parts of whole shapes which are fractions but also also by providing examples which are not. In the case of the circle whole, non-exemplars in the form of 'slices' are used. Examples of circle slices are shown on the next page.

Slices are slightly easier to plot in graphics because only one PLOT and one LINE instruction in BASIC is required per slice, instead of two for circle sectors. An example of a section of BASIC code which draws a horizontal slice of a circle subdivided into 4 parts of equal height with centre (150,150) (as in the bottom left hand illustration on the next page) is :

```
10 CALL "CIRCLE" 16,48,150,150,3
20 CALL "PLOT" 128,105,3:CALL "LINE
172,105,3
```

F=128;X=128,Y=105   S=16;X=172,Y=105

Circle 'slices' which are not fractional parts of whole Circles

MOVING CIRCLE SECTORS
'FLASHING'

Circle sectors may be 'turned on and off' (flashed) at suitable speed by first setting the intensity argument to white to 'turn the shape on ' and from the *BASIC* program calling circle, plot and line with the appropriate arguments to draw a sector of appropriate size, angle and centre co-ordinates. Next, after a suitable delay if necessary, precisely the same instructions are repeated except to set the intensity argument to black (N=0), which effectively 'turns the shape off'. This procedure is repeated an appropriate number of times- about 10 times was found to be best in practice, the idea being to draw the observer's attention to the sector. The block of *BASIC* code finishes by drawing the sector in white again. In the example on the next page, *BASIC* instructions are used to flash the 1/3 circle sector shown at the top left on p. 105.

Section of a BASIC program to 'flash' a 1/3 circle sector

10 FORI=1 TO 10

20 N=3:GOSUB 41000:GOSUB 50000:N=0:GOSUB 41000

30 NEXT I

40 N=3:GOSUB 41000

.

.

.

41000 CALL "CIRCLE" 32,75,X,Y,N:CALL "PLOT" X-43,Y-25,N:CALL "LINE" X,Y:
CALL "LINE" X,Y+50:RETURN

50000 FOR P=1 TO 100:NEXT P

41100 CALL "CIRCLE" 117,128,X,Y,N:"CIRCLE" 0,32,X,Y,N:CALL "PLOT" X+43,Y-25,N:
CALL "LINE" X,Y:CALL "LINE" X,Y+50:RETURN

41200 CALL "CIRCLE" 75,117,X,Y,N:CALL "PLOT" X-43,Y-25,N:CALL "LINE" X,Y:
CALL "LINE" X+43,Y-25:CALL "LINE":RETURN

50000 FOR Q=1 TO P:NEXT Q:RETURN

ROTATION

Rotation of a circle sector on the graphics screen can be achieved by first drawing the circle sector in white as described above. Next, again after programming in a suitable delay, using the same S,F,X and Y arguments, the intensity argument N is set to black, the circle subroutine is called again, which effectively 'erases' it on the graphics screen. Then the arguments S and F are changed, keeping the *difference* between their values the same, which effectively turns the arc through an angle, calling the circle subroutine once again, with N set for white. The plot and line subroutine arguments have also to be changed appropriately. For example, the three subroutines 41000, 41100 and 41200 on p. 113 can be used to rotate a 1/3 circle sector from the position shown at the top left of the illustration on p. 105 to the position shown at the centre, bottom. A section of *BASIC* code to do this is on the next page.

Example of a BASIC program segment to rotate a circle sector

```
10 Y=100:P=100

20 N=3:GOSUB 41000:GOSUB 50000:N=0:GOSUB 41000:GOSUB 50000

30 N=3:GOSUB 41100:GOSUB 50000:N=0:GOSUB 41100:GOSUB 50000

40 N=3:GOSUB 41200
```

.
.
.

```
41000 CALL "CIRCLE" 32,75,X,Y,N:CALL "PLOT" X-43,Y-25,N:CALL "LINE" X,Y:
CALL "LINE" X,Y+50:CALL "LINE":RETURN

41100 CALL "CIRCLE" 117,128,X,Y,N:"CIRCLE" 0,32,X,Y,N:CALL "PLOT" X+43,Y-25,N:
CALL "LINE" X,Y:CALL "LINE" X,Y+50:RETURN

41200 CALL "CIRCLE" 75,117,X,Y,N:CALL "PLOT" X-43,Y-25,N:CALL "LINE" X,Y:
CALL "LINE" X+43,Y-25:CALL "LINE":RETURN

50000  FOR Q=1 TO P:NEXT Q:RETURN
```

TRANSLATION

Circle sectors were translated on the graphics screen by first drawing the sector in white, using appropriate arguments with the "circle", "plot" and "line" subroutines as described above. Then, after a suitable delay, identical instructions, except that intensity arguments were set to black, 'erased' the sector. Next, after another suitable delay, the sector was drawn in a new position in white and then black, as before. This is continued in suitable steps until the sector reaches its destination- being left drawn in white.

Suitable delays are introduced if required to prevent the circle sector from 'moving' too rapidly for the eye to follow its trajectory. This was achieved using a FOR-NEXT loop, whose parameters could be adjusted to execute the loop a given number of times to set the amount of the delay as required. In practice, around 100 was found to be suitable.

An example of a section of *BASIC* code which translates the circle 1/3 sector on p. 105 from centre (100,100) to (200,100) in steps of 20 is shown on the next page.

Example of a BASIC program segment to translate a circle sector

10 Y=100:P=100

20 FOR X=100 TO 200 STEP 20

30 N=0:GOSUB 41000

40 GOSUB 50000

50 N=1:GOSUB 41000

60 NEXT I

70 N=3: GOSUB 41000

.

.

41000 CALL "CIRCLE" 32,75,X,Y,N:CALL "PLOT" X-43,Y-25,N:CALL "LINE" X,Y:
CALL "LINE" X,Y+50:CALL "LINE":RETURN

50000 FOR Q=1 TO P:NEXT Q:RETURN

THE OTHER (NON-CIRCLE) SHAPES

The other shapes are a rectangle- a thin rectangle or 'rod' 100 x 10 pixels and a square of side 100 pixels, together with fractional (and non-fractional) parts of these whole shapes.

These are straightforwardly produced using sequences of PLOT and LINE instructions in *BASIC*. For example, a horizontal rod with its bottom left hand corner at 50,50 is built up as follows:

10 CALL "PLOT" 50,50,3

20 CALL "LINE" 150,50

_____

(50,50)   (150,50)

30 CALL "LINE" 150,40

_____

40 CALL "LINE" 50,40

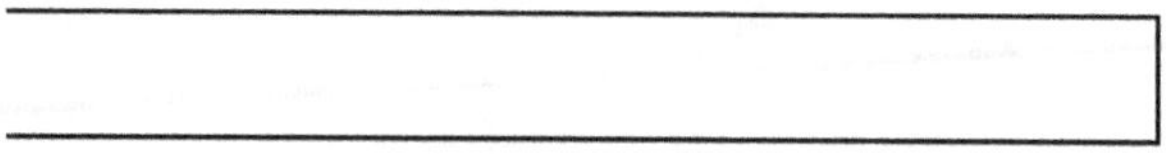

_____

50 CALL "LINE" 50,50

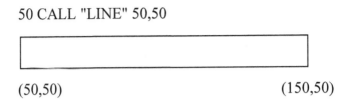

(50,50)   (150,50)

Different orientations are obtained by changing the X,Y arguments of PLOT and LINE appropriately. For example a vertical rod bottom left hand corner at 150,150 is produced by

10 CALL "PLOT" 150,150,3
20 CALL "LINE" 160,150
30 CALL "LINE" 160,50
40 CALL "LINE" 150,50
50 CALL "LINE" 150,150

150,50   160,50

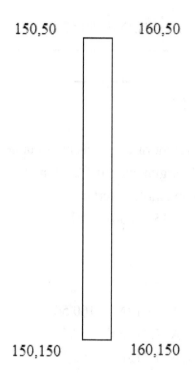

150,150   160,150

However, programming is simplified if a *BASIC* subroutine is used consisting of a PLOT and four LINE instructions whose X and Y arguments are variables instead of fixed values. This allows any rectangular shape, including the rod and parts of the rod and the square and parts of the square, to be drawn in any orientation anywhere on the graphics screen. An example of such a subroutine is:

```
40000  CALL  "PLOT"  A,B,N:CALL  "LINE"
C,B:CALL"LINE"C,D:CALL "LINE" A,D:
CALL "LINE"A,B:RETURN
```

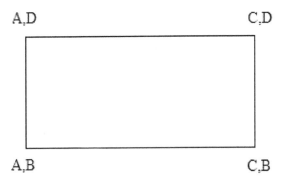

Two examples will be given illustrated from copies of original print-outs from sections of the BASIC graphics teaching program. The first is shown on the next page. The results are shown below

A,D   C,D

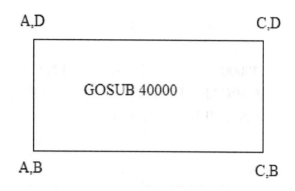

GOSUB 40000

A,B   C,B

Line 120

107,176   207,176

107,166   207,166

14,100   64,100   250,100   300,100

14,90   64,90   250,90   300,90

(The lines 14-300 draw a large '1/2' symbols in graphics)

Print-out of a section of code from the BASIC graphics teaching program illustrating 1/2s of the 'rod' whole shape

The next print-out on p. 122 is of a section of *BASIC* code which draws 1/4s of the rod as follows:

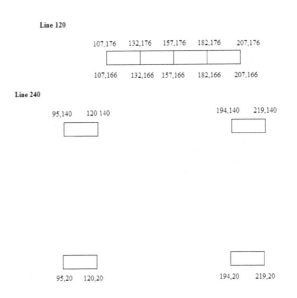

(lines 140-220 are concerned with drawing a large graphics '1/4' symbol)

Flashing, rotation and translating are achieved using the same *BASIC* programming techniques as explained in the case of the circle and so will not be described in detail here.

Print-out of a section of code from the BASIC graphics teaching program illustrating 1/4s of the 'rod' whole shape

```
Ready:
?

Ready:
LOAD"C:IP1S2"

Ready:
LIST_

100 CALL"RESOLUTION",0,2
120 N=3:A=107:B=176:C=207:D=166:GOSUB40000:C=132:GOSUB40000:C=157:GOSUB40000:C=182:G
=2:Y=146:A$="1":N1=2:X=152
140 GOSUB30400:FORI=0TO4:CALL"PLOT",155+I,135:CALL"LINE",155+I,95:NEXTI
160 FORI=0TO4:CALL"PLOT",127,90-I:CALL"LINE",187,90-I:NEXTI
180 FORI=0TO4:CALL"PLOT",155+I,80:CALL"LINE",155+I,35:NEXTI
200 FORI=0TO4:CALL"PLOT",155,80-I:CALL"LINE",130+I,50:NEXTI
220 FORI=0TO4:CALL"PLOT",130,50-I:CALL"LINE",170,50-I:NEXTI
240 A=95:C=120:B=140:D=130:GOSUB40000:A=194:C=219:GOSUB40000:B=30:D=20:GOSUB40000:A=
UB40000
250 LOADGO"PIS2M1"
2000 STOP
30400 CALL"CHARSIZE",N1,N1:CALL"STPLOT",X,Y,VARADR(A$),N:RETURN
40000 CALL"PLOT",A,B,N:CALL"LINE",C,B:CALL"LINE",C,D:CALL"LINE",A,D:CALL"LINE",A,B:R

Ready:
```

9. CONCLUSION

The development of a machine code program to draw a circle and circle segments for the *Zilog Z80* microprocessor-based *Research Machines 380Z* microcomputer has been described. The purpose of the machine code program was to draw circles and circle segments at sufficient speed to 'move' them around the graphics screen, to flash them and rotate them as part of a graphics teaching program in *BASIC*.

BASIC itself, a high level programming language, was inadequate to this task. A circle of the required size involved plotting at least 352 points. So the PLOT subroutine had to be called from *BASIC* 352 times to draw each complete circle, after the 704 co-ordinates of the points were calculated by applying sine and cosine functions up to 256 times and mathematically reflecting in the X and Y axes to generate the 4 quadrants.

Programming began in assembly language (ASM), which, consisting of mnemonics and labels instead of binary instructions and memory address, simplified the process of deciding on the logic the machine program would use in order to achieve its purpose. This could then be translated into binary machine code instructions and these into hexadecimal values for installation and execution from within a *BASIC* program written for this purpose.

After familiarisation with the structure and functions of the Z80- its 'architecture'- the registers including accumulator, program counter and flag registers, the stack and memory, which all feature in ASM programming, the first stage of program development therefore was to choose those mnemonic instructions which were to be used in program development (the list of which could be added to as program development progressed) and then to become familiar in practice with assembly language lexicon- the mnemonic instructions, and the syntax- the rules for using and combining the mnemonics. This was achieved via 6 programs of increasing complexity, starting with a simple ASM program to add two numbers, which was then progressively extended to include additional programming facilities -progressing from the simplest situation where the operands are pre-loaded into registers then loading from locations in memory to use of the stack storage area, testing results for zero using the accumulator and compare instructions, multiplication, and the use of the auxiliary set of registers on the Z80- facilities which would ultimately be required in the circle machine code program.

The next step was to translate each ASM mnemonic instruction, the operation carried out and the operands to which the operation was applied, into binary code using the *Z80*'s 'instruction set'.

The binary code was converted into hexadecimal, which would result in a much more manageable and compact program far less tedious and error prone to install. The hexadecimal codes could then installed in memory using *BASIC*.

The next step in program development was therefore choice of and familiarisation with the programming features and instructions in *BASIC* which could be used to install and execute a machine language program. The hexadecimal codes were installed in memory with POKE commands. Mindful that 700 or more bytes for the data of the program alone would have to be installed each requiring a POKE command, the use of multiple input and output data of the file feature in BASIC was investigated, followed by FOR-NEXT loops to read the data in and out of a DATA file, with each datum as the argument of a POKE instruction.

The writing of a program in *BASIC* to install and execute the machine code program also required the use of a number of other 'book-keeping' features of *BASIC*, including line numbering of statements, suitable choice of memory area and the clearing of sufficient space for the program in computer memory, preventing the program from being overwritten; CALLing the program; returning to *BASIC* after execution; and RUNning the *BASIC* program.

Adding in all the necessary book-keeping functions, a complete *BASIC* program on the *380 Z* was produced to install and execute a program to add two numbers, which had been previously developed in assembly language then converted into hex machine code, as the final stepping stone onto the more complex graphics program development.

This began with a program to plot a single 'pixel' or graphics dot, moving on to a program to plot all the dots necessary to display a full circle and finally the full program which plots a circle or part of a circle with centre co-ordinates defined by the user.

The stages involved may be summarised as follow:

(1) Use the cache memory area 0-7BFF H above CP/M, determining the start and finish addresses of the block of memory to be used for the machine code graphics program with the *BASIC* CLEAR instruction

(2) Write the assembly language program

(3) Convert the ASM mnemonics into op. codes

(4) Write the data list for the points in hex using the *BASIC* DATA instruction

(5) Read (4) into the chosen memory locations using the *BASIC* PEEK instruction with a FOR-NEXT loop beginning Endmem+1, where Endmem is the starting address of the block of memory reserved for the machine code program.

(6) CALL the machine code start address in memory from *BASIC*

(7) Include all the necessary book-keeping instructions as described to install the machine code program in memory

(8) RUN the program using the instruction loadgo

Each pixel was plotted using a call to the built in "PLOT" subroutine in *BASIC*. Once a successful program to plot a single pixel had been achieved, the way was cleared for a program which would plot all the graphics points necessary to display a full circle. The co-ordinates of the points were determined using sine and cosine functions, saving them in a DATA file. They were then installed in memory using POKE statements. Without calculating the co-ordinates each time, these could be fetched from memory by a machine code program and plotted. The program was speeded up by including instructions to reject about 1/3 of all the pairs of co-ordinates in the DATA file which represented repeated points.

The previous program was then extended so that a circle or part of a circle of radius 50 could be plotted in black or white anywhere on the screen as determined by user-supplied arguments values for the start and finish points of the part of the circle required, arguments for the co-ordinates of the circle centre and an intensity (colour) argument.

To enable the user to pass the appropriate arguments to the program, a "CALL" in BASIC with the 5 arguments was included in the program instructions.

Finally, a subroutine (loop) of extra instructions to multiply the start (S) and finish (F) addresses of the desired circle arc by 8 prior to further processing by the program was included to appropriately transform the argument values in the finished "CIRCLE" S,F,X,Y,N call to the machine code program from *BASIC*.

The final chapter described the use of the program to generate 'moving' graphics shapes which featured in a graphics-based teaching program written in *BASIC*. This included simple fractional parts of the circle or circle sectors and 'slices', and also 'flashing', rotation and translation. Since the teaching program was based on thin rectangular and square shapes as well as circular, the programming techniques used to produce the former were also outlined.

11. APPENDICES

APPENDIX 1: Z80 INSTRUCTION CODE SUBSET

8-Bit Load Group

LD r, r'

Operation: $r_1 \leftarrow r_2$

Op Code: LD

Operands: r, r'

0	1	← r₁ →	← r₂ →

Description: The contents of any register r_2 are loaded to any other register r_1. r_1, r_2 identifies any of the registers A, B, C, D, E, H, or L, assembled as follows in the object code:

Register	r, C
A	111
B	000
C	001
D	010
E	011
H	100
L	101

Example: If the H register contains the number 8AH, and the E register contains 10H, the instruction LD H, E results in both registers containing 10H.

LD r,n

Operation: $r \leftarrow n$

Op Code: LD

Operands: r, n

0	0	← r →	1	1	0
←			n		→

Description: The 8-bit integer n is loaded to any register r, where r identifies register A, B, C, D, E, H, or L, assembled as follows in the object code:

Register	r
A	111
B	000
C	001
D	010
E	011
H	100
L	101

Example: At execution of LD E, A5H the contents of register E are A5H.

134

LD r, (HL)

Operation: r ← (HL)

Op Code: LD

Operands: r, (HL)

| 0 | 1 | ◄— | r | —► | 1 | 1 | 0 |

Description: The 8-bit contents of memory location (HL) are loaded to register r, where r identifies register A, B, C, D, E, H, or L, assembled as follows in the object code:

Register	r
A	111
B	000
C	001
D	010
E	011
H	100
L	101

Example: If register pair HL contains the number 75A1H, and memory address 75A1H contains byte 58H, the execution of LD C, (HL) results in 58H in register C.

LD (HL), r

Operation: (HL) ← r

Op Code: LD

Operands: (HL), r

| 0 | 1 | 1 | 1 | 0 | ◄— | r | —► |

Description: The contents of register r are loaded to the memory location specified by the contents of the HL register pair. The symbol r identifies register A, B, C, D, E, H, or L, assembled as follows in the object code:

Register	r
A	111
B	000
C	001
D	010
E	011
H	100
L	101

Example: If the contents of register pair HL specifies memory location 2146H, and the B register contains byte 29H, at execution of LD (HL), B memory address 2146H also contains 29H.

LD (HL), n

Operation: (HL) ← n

Op Code: LD

Operands: (HL), n

0	0	1	1	0	1	1	0	36

				n				

Description: Integer n is loaded to the memory address specified by the contents of the HL register pair.

Example: If the HL register pair contains 4444H, the instruction LD (HL), 28H results in the memory location 4444H containing byte 28H.

LD A, (BC)

Operation: A ← (BC)

Op Code: LD

Operands: A, (BC)

0	0	0	0	1	0	1	0	0A

Description: The contents of the memory location specified by the contents of the BC register pair are loaded to the Accumulator.

Example: If the BC register pair contains the number 4747H, and memory address 4747H contains byte 12H, then the instruction LD A, (BC) results in byte 12H in register A.

LD A, (DE)

Operation: A ← (DE)

Op Code: LD

Operands: A. (DE)

0	0	0	1	1	0	1	0	1A

Description: The contents of the memory location specified by the register pair DE are loaded to the Accumulator.

Example: If the DE register pair contains the number 30A2H and memory address 30A2H contains byte 22H, then the instruction LD A, (DE) results in byte 22H in register A.

LD A, (nn)

Operation: A ← (nn)

Op Code: LD

Operands: A, (nn)

0	0	1	1	1	0	1	0	3A

◄─────── n ───────►

◄─────── n ───────►

Description: The contents of the memory location specified by the operands nn are loaded to the Accumulator. The first n operand after the Op Code is the low order byte of a 2-byte memory address.

Example: If the contents of nn is number 8832H, and the content of memory address 8832H is byte 04H, at instruction LD A, (nn) byte 04H is in the Accumulator.

LD (BC), A

Operation: (BC) ← A

Op Code: LD

Operands: (BC), A

0	0	0	0	0	0	1	0	02

Description: The contents of the Accumulator are loaded to the memory location specified by the contents of the register pair BC.

Example: If the Accumulator contains 7AH and the BC register pair contains 1212H the instruction LD (BC), A results in 7AH in memory location 1212H.

LD (DE), A

Operation: (DE) ← A

Op Code: LD

Operands: (DE), A

0	0	0	1	0	0	1	0	12

Description: The contents of the Accumulator are loaded to the memory location specified by the contents of the DE register pair.

Example: If the contents of register pair DE are 1128H, and the Accumulator contains byte A0H, the instruction LD (DE), A results in A0H in memory location 1128H.

LD (nn), A

Operation: (nn) ← A

Op Code: LD

Operands: (nn), A

0	0	1	1	0	0	1	0	32

◄——————— n ———————►

◄——————— n ———————►

Description: The contents of the Accumulator are loaded to the memory address specified by the operand nn. The first n operand after the Op Code is the low order byte of nn.

Example: If the contents of the Accumulator are byte D7H, at execution of LD (3141 H), AD7H results in memory location 3141H.

16-Bit Load Group

LD dd, nn

Operation: dd ← nn

Op Code: LD

Operands: dd, nn

0	0	d	d	0	0	0	1

◄——————— n ———————►

◄——————— n ———————►

Description: The 2-byte integer nn is loaded to the dd register pair, where dd defines the BC, DE, HL, or SP register pairs, assembled as follows in the object code:

Pair	dd
BC	00
DE	01
HL	10
SP	11

Example: At execution of LD HL, 5000H the contents of the HL register pair is 5000H.

LD HL, (nn)

Operation: $H \leftarrow (nn+1), L \leftarrow (nn)$

Op Code: LD

Operands: HL, (nn)

0	0	1	0	1	0	1	0	2A

←			n			→

←			n			→

Description: The contents of memory address (nn) are loaded to the low order portion of register pair HL (register L), and the contents of the next highest memory address (nn+1) are loaded to the high order portion of HL (register H). The first n operand after the Op Code is the low order byte of nn.

Example: If address 4545H contains 37H, and address 4546H contains A1H, at instruction LD HL, (4545H) the HL register pair contains A137H.

LD dd, (nn)

Operation: $ddh \leftarrow (nn+1) \; ddl \leftarrow (nn)$

Op Code: LD

Operands: dd, (nn)

1	1	1	0	1	1	0	1	ED

0	1	d	d	1	0	1	1

←			n			→

←			n			→

Description: The contents of address (nn) are loaded to the low order portion of register pair dd, and the contents of the next highest memory address (nn+1) are loaded to the high order portion of dd. Register pair dd defines BC, DE, HL, or SP register pairs, assembled as follows in the object code:

Pair	dd
BC	00
DE	01
HL	10
SP	11

Example: If Address 2130H contains 65H, and address 2131M contains 78H, at instruction LD BC, (2130H) the BC register pair contains 7865H.

LD (nn), HL

Operation: (nn+1) ← H, (nn) ← L

Op Code: LD

Operands: (nn), HL

0	0	1	0	0	0	1	0	22

←			n			→

←			n			→

Description: The contents of the low order portion of register pair HL (register L) are loaded to memory address (nn), and the contents of the high order portion of HL (register H) are loaded to the next highest memory address (nn+1). The first n operand after the Op Code is the low order byte of nn.

Example: If the content of register pair HL is 483AH, at instruction LD (B2291-1), HL address B229H contains 3AH, and address B22AH

LD (nn), dd

Operation: (nn+1) ← ddh, (nn) ← ddl

Op Code: LD

Operands: (nn), dd

1	1	1	0	1	1	0	1	ED

0	1	d	d	0	0	1	1

←			n			→

←			n			→

Description: The low order byte of register pair dd is loaded to memory address (nn); the upper byte is loaded to memory address (nn+1). Register pair dd defines either BC, DE, HL, or SP, assembled as follows in the object code:

Pair	dd
BC	00
DE	01
HL	10
SP	11

Example: If register pair BC contains the number 4644H, the instruction LD (1000H), BC results in 44H in memory location 1000H, and 46H in memory location 1001H.

PUSH qq

Operation: $(SP-2) \leftarrow qqL, (SP-1) \leftarrow qqH$

Op Code: PUSH

Operands: qq

1	1	q	q	0	1	0	1

Description: The contents of the register pair qq are pushed to the external memory LIFO (last-in, first-out) Stack. The Stack Pointer (SP) register pair holds the 16-bit address of the current top of the Stack. This instruction first decrements SP and loads the high order byte of register pair qq to the memory address specified by the SP. The SP is decremented again and loads the low order byte of qq to the memory location corresponding to this new address in the SP. The operand qq identifies register pair BC, DE, HL, or AF, assembled as follows in the object code:

Pair	qq
BC	00
DE	01
HL	10
AF	11

Example: If the AF register pair contains 2233H and the Stack Pointer contains 1007H, at instruction PUSH AF memory address 1006H contains 22H, memory address 1005H contains 33H, and the Stack Pointer contains 1005H.

POP qq

Operation: $qqH \leftarrow (SP+1), qqL \leftarrow (SP)$

Op Code: POP

Operands: qq

1	1	q	q	0	0	0	1

Description: The top two bytes of the external memory LIFO (last-in, first-out) Stack are popped to register pair qq. The Stack Pointer (SP) register pair holds the 16-bit address of the current top of the Stack. This instruction first loads to the low order portion of qq, the byte at memory location corresponding to the contents of SP; then SP is incriminated and the contents of the corresponding adjacent memory location are loaded to the high order portion of qq and the SP is now incriminated again. The operand qq identifies register pair BC, DE, HL, or AF, assembled as follows in the object code:

Pair	r
BC	00
DE	01
HL	10
AF	11

Example: If the Stack Pointer contains 1000H, memory location 1000H contains 55H, and location 1001H contains 33H, the instruction POP HL results in register pair HL containing 3355H, and the Stack Pointer containing 1002H.

EX DE, HL

Operation: DE ↔ HL

Op Code: EX

Operands: DE, HL

1	1	1	0	1	0	1	1	EB

Description: The 2-byte contents of register pairs DE and HL are exchanged.

Example: If the content of register pair DE is the number 2822H, and the content of the register pair HL is number 499AH, at instruction EX DE, HL the content of register pair DE is 499AH, and the content of register pair HL is 2822H.

EXX

Operation: (BC) ↔ (BC'), (DE) ↔ (DE'), (HL) ↔ (HL')

Op Code: EXX

Operands: —

1	1	0	1	1	0	0	0	D9

Description: Each 2-byte value in register pairs BC, DE, and HL is exchanged with the 2-byte value in BC', DE', and HL', respectively.

Example: If the contents of register pairs BC, DE, and HL are the numbers 445AH, 3DA2H, and 8859H, respectively, and the contents of register pairs BC', DE', and HL' are 0988H, 9300H, and 00E7H, respectively, at instruction EXX the contents of the register pairs are as follows: BC' contains 0988H; DE' contains 9300H; HL contains 00E7H; BC' contains 445AH; DE' contains 3DA2H; and HL' contains 8859H.

8-Bit Arithmetic Group

ADD A, r

Operation: $A \leftarrow A + r$

Op Code: ADD

Operands: A, r

1	0	0	0	0	← r →

Description: The contents of register r are added to the contents of the Accumulator, and the result is stored in the Accumulator. The symbol r identifies the registers A, B, C, D, E, H, or L, assembled as follows in the object code:

Register	r
A	111
B	000
C	001
D	010
E	011
H	100
L	101

Z is set if result is zero; reset otherwise   C is set if carry from bit 7; reset otherwise

Example: If the contents of the Accumulator are 44H, and the contents of register C are 11H, at execution of ADD A,C the contents of the Accumulator are 55H.

ADD A, n

Operation: $A \leftarrow A + n$

Op Code: ADD

Operands: A, n

1	1	0	0	0	1	1	0	C6
←			n			→		

Description: The integer n is added to the contents of the Accumulator, and the results are stored in the Accumulator.

Z is set if result is zero; reset otherwise   C is set if carry from bit 7; reset otherwise

Example: If the contents of the Accumulator are 23H, at execution of ADD A, 33H the contents of the Accumulator are 56H.

ADD A, (HL)

Operation: A ← A + (HL)

Op Code: ADD

Operands: A, (HL)

1	0	0	0	0	1	1	0	86

Description: The byte at the memory address specified by the contents of the HL register pair is added to the contents of the Accumulator, and the result is stored in the Accumulator.

Z is set if result is zero; reset otherwise   C is set if carry from bit 7; reset otherwise

Example: If the contents of the Accumulator are A0H, and the content of the register pair HL is 2323H, and memory location 2323H contains byte 08H, at execution of ADD A, (HL) the Accumulator contains A8H.

ADC A, s

Operation: A ← A + s + CY

Z is set if result is zero; reset otherwise

Op Code: ADC

C is set if carry from bit 7; reset otherwise

Operands: A, s

This s operand is any of r, n, (HL)

ADC A,r

1	0	0	0	1	←	← r* →	→

ADC A,n

1	1	0	0	1	1	1	0	CE

←				n			→

ADC A, (HL)

1	0	0	0	1	1	1	0	8E

*r identifies registers B, C, D, E, H, L, or A assembled as follows in the object code field above

Register	r
B	000
C	001
D	010
E	011
H	100
L	101
A	111

Example: If the Accumulator contents are 16H, the Carry Flag is set, the HL register pair contains 6666H, and address 6666H contains 10H, at execution of ADC A, (HL) the Accumulator contains 27H.

CP s

Operation: A - s   Z is set if result is zero; reset otherwise

Op Code: CP

Operands: s

The s operand is any of r, n, (HL).

CP r*	1	0	1	1	1	◄— r* —►		

CP n	1	1	1	1	1	1	1	0	FE

◄—			n			—►

CP (HL)	1	0	1	1	1	1	1	0	BE

*r identifies registers B, C, D, E, H, L, or A specified as follows in the assembled object code field above:

Register	r
B	000
C	001
D	010
E	011
H	100
L	101
A	111

INC r

Operation: r ← r + 1

Op Code: INC

Operands: r

0	0	◄— r —►	1	0	0

Description: Register r is incremented and register r identifies any of the registers A, B, C, D, E, H, or L, assembled as follows in the object code.

Register	r
A	111
B	000
C	001
D	010
E	011
H	100
L	101

Example: If the contents of register D are 28H, at execution of INC D the contents of register D are 29H.

DEC m

Operation: $m \leftarrow m-1$

Op Code: DEC

Operands: m

The m operand is any of r, (HL)

DEC r*	0	0	←	r	→	1	0	1

DEC (HL)	0	0	1	1	0	1	0	1	35

*r identifies registers B, C, D, E, H, L, or A object code field above:

Register	r
B	000
C	001
D	010
E	011
H	100
L	101
A	111

Example: If the D register contains byte 2AH, at execution of DEC D register D contains 29H.

16-Bit Arithmetic Group

ADD HL, ss

Operation: $HL \leftarrow HL + ss$

Op Code: ADD

Operands: HL, ss

0	0	s	s	1	0	0	1

Description: The contents of register pair ss (any of register pairs BC, DE, HL, or SP) are added to the contents of register pair HL and the result is stored in HL. Operand ss is specified as follows in the assembled object code.

Register Pair	ss
BC	00
DE	01
HL	10
SP	11

Example: If register pair HL contains the integer 4242H, and register pair DE contains 1111H, at execution of ADD HL, DE the HL register pair contains 5353H.

ADC HL, ss

Operation: HL ← HL + ss + CY

Op Code: ADC

Operands: IIL. ss

1	1	1	0	1	1	0	1	ED

0	1	s	s	1	0	1	0

Description: The contents of register pair ss (any of register pairs BC, DE, HL, or SP) are added with the Carry flag (C flag in the F register) to the contents of register pair HL, and the result is stored in HL. Operand ss is specified as follows in the assembled object code.

Register Pair	ss
BC	00
DE	01
HL	10
SP	11

Example: If the register pair BC contains 2222H, register pair HL contains 5437H, and the Carry Flag is set, at execution of ADC HL, BC the contents of HL are 765AH.

INC ss

Operation: ss ← ss + 1

Op Code: INC

Operands: ss

0	0	s	s	0	0	1	1

Description: The contents of register pair ss (any of register pairs BC, DE, HL, or SP) are incremented. Operand ss is specified as follows in the assembled object code.

Register Pair	ss
BC	00
DE	01
HL	10
SP	11

Example: If the register pair contains 1000H, after the execution of INC HL, HL contains 1001H.

SLA m

Operation:

$$CY \leftarrow \boxed{7 \leftarrow \quad \leftarrow 0} \leftarrow 0$$
$$m$$

Z is set if result is zero; reset otherwise
C is data from bit 7

Op Code: SLA

Operands: m

The m operand is any of r   SLA r* | 1 | 1 | 0 | 0 | 1 | 0 | 1 | 1 | CB

*r identifies registers B, C, D, E, H, L, or A assembled as follows in the object code field above:

Register	r
B	000
C	001
D	010
E	011
H	100
L	101
A	111

Example: If the contents of register L are

7	6	5	4	3	2	1	0
1	0	1	1	0	0	0	1

at execution of SLA L the contents of register L and the Carry flag are

C	7	6	5	4	3	2	1	0
1	0	1	1	0	0	0	1	0

RES b, m

Operation: $sb \leftarrow 0$

Op Code: RES

Operands: b, m

Operand b is any bit (7 through 0) of the contents of the m operand, (any of r, (HL)

RES b, m | 1 | 1 | 0 | 0 | 1 | 0 | 1 | 1 | CB
          | 1 | 0 | ← b → | ← r → |

RES b, (HL) | 1 | 1 | 0 | 0 | 1 | 0 | 1 | 1 | CB
             | 1 | 0 | ← b → | 1 | 1 | 0 |

Example: At execution of RES 6, D, bit 6 in register 0 resets. Bit 0 in register D is the least-significant bit.

Bit	b	Register	r
0	000	B	000
1	001	C	001
2	010	D	010
3	011	E	011
4	100	H	100
5	101	L	101
6	110	A	111
7	111		

Jump Group

JP nn

Operation: PC ← nn

Op Code: JP

Operands: nn

1	1	0	0	0	0	1	1	C3

← n →

← n →

Note: The first operand in this assembled object code is the low order byte of a two-byte address.

Description: Operand nn is loaded to register pair PC (Program Counter). The next instruction is fetched from the location designated by the new contents of the PC.

JP cc, nn

Operation: IF cc true, PC ← nn

Op Code: JP

Operands: cc, nn

1	1	←	00	→	0	1	0

← n →

← n →

Example:
If the Carry flag (C flag in the F register) is set and the contents of address 1520 are 03H, at execution of JP C, 1520H the Program Counter contains 1520H, and on the next machine cycle the CPD fetches byte 03H from address 1520H.

The first n operand in this assembled object code is the low order byte of a 2-byte memory address.

Description: If condition cc is true, the instruction loads operand nn to register pair PC (Program Counter), and the program continues with the instruction beginning at address nn. If condition cc is false, the Program Counter is incremented as usual, and the program continues with the next sequential instruction. Condition cc is programmed as one of eight status that corresponds to condition bits in the Flag Register (register F).

cc	Condition	Flag				
000	NZ non zero	Z	010	NC no carry	C
001	Z zero	Z	011	C carry	C

JR e

Operation: PC ← PC + e

Op Code: JR

Operands: e

0	0	0	1	1	0	0	0	18

←				e-2				→

Description: This instruction provides for unconditional branching to other segments of a program. The value of the displacement e is added to the Program Counter (PC) and the next instruction is fetched from the location designated by the new contents of the PC. This jump is measured from the address of the instruction Op Code and has a range of -126 to +129 bytes. The assembler automatically adjusts for the twice incremented PC.

JR Z, e

Operation: If Z = 0, continue
               If Z = 1, PC ← PC +e

Op Code: JR

Operands: Z, e

0	0	1	0	1	0	0	0	28

←				e-2				→

Description: This instruction provides for conditional branching to other segments of a program depending on the results of a test on the Zero Flag. If the flag is equal to a 1, the value of the displacement e is added to the Program Counter (PC) and the next instruction is fetched from the location designated by the new contents of the PC. The jump is measured from the address of the instruction Op Code and has a range of -126 to +129 bytes. The assembler automatically adjusts for the twice incremented PC.

If the Zero Flag is equal to a 0, the next instruction executed is taken from the location following this instruction. If the condition is met:

JR NZ, e

Operation: If Z = 1, continue
If Z = 0, PC ← pc + e

Op Code: JR

Operands: NZ, e

0	0	1	0	0	0	0	0	20

←				e-2			→	

Description: This instruction provides for conditional branching to other segments of a program depending on the results of a test on the Zero Flag. If the flag is equal to a 0, the value of the displacement e is added to the Program Counter (PC) and the next instruction is fetched from the location designated by the new contents of the PC. The jump is measured from the address of the instruction Op Code and has a range of -126 to +129 bytes. The assembler automatically adjusts for the twice incremented PC.

If the Zero Flag is equal to a 1, the next instruction executed is taken from the location following this instruction.

RET

Operation: pCL ← (sp), pCH ← (sp+1)

Op Code: RET

1	1	0	0	1	0	0	1	C9

Description: The byte at the memory location specified by the contents of the Stack Pointer (SP) register pair is moved to the low order eight bits of the Program Counter (PC). The SP is now incremented and the byte at the memory location specified by the new contents of this instruction is fetched from the memory location specified by the PC. This instruction is normally used to return to the main line program at the completion of a routine entered by a CALL instruction.

Example: If the contents of the Program Counter are 3535H, the contents of the Stack Pointer are 2000H, the contents of memory location 2000H are B5H, and the contents of memory location of memory location 2001H are 18H. At execution of RET the contents of the Stack Pointer is 2002H, and the contents of the Program Counter is 18B5H, pointing to the address of the next program Op Code to be fetched.

APPENDIX 2: BINARY TO DECIMAL CONVERSION TABLE:

To convert from binary to hexadecimal, use Appendix 2 to convert binary to decimal and then Appendix 3 to convert decimal to hexadecimal.

Low Byte

	0000	0001	0010	0011	0100	0101	0110	0111	1000	1001	1010	1011	1100	1101	1110	1111
0000	0	1	2	3	4	5	6	7	8	9	10	11	12	13	14	15
0001	16	17	18	19	20	21	22	23	24	25	26	27	28	29	30	31
0010	32	33	34	35	36	37	38	39	40	41	42	43	44	45	46	47
0011	48	49	50	51	52	53	54	55	56	57	58	59	60	61	62	63
0100	64	65	66	67	68	69	70	71	72	73	74	75	76	77	78	79
0101	80	81	82	83	84	85	86	87	88	89	90	91	92	93	94	95
0110	96	97	98	99	100	101	102	103	104	105	106	107	108	109	110	111
0111	112	113	114	115	116	117	118	119	120	121	122	123	124	125	126	127
1000	128	129	130	131	132	133	134	135	136	137	138	139	140	141	142	143
1001	144	145	146	147	148	149	150	151	152	153	154	155	156	157	158	159
1010	160	161	162	163	164	165	166	167	168	169	170	171	172	173	174	175

154

1011	176	177	178	179	180	181	182	183	184	185	186	187	188	189	190	191
1100	192	193	194	195	196	197	198	199	200	201	202	203	204	205	206	207
1101	208	209	210	211	212	213	214	215	216	217	218	219	220	221	222	223
1110	224	225	226	227	228	229	230	231	232	233	234	235	236	237	238	239
1111	240	241	242	243	244	245	246	247	248	249	250	251	252	253	254	255

High Byte

0000 0001 0000 0000	256
0000 0010 0000 0000	512
0000 0100 0000 0000	1024
0000 1000 0000 0000	2048
0001 0000 0000 0000	4096
0010 0000 0000 0000	8192
0100 0000 0000 0000	16384
1000 0000 0000 0000	32768

APPENDIX 3: HEXADECIMAL TO DECIMAL CONVERSION TABLE

	0	1	2	3	4	5	6	7	8	9	A	B	C	D	E	F
00	000	001	002	003	004	005	006	007	008	009	010	011	012	013	014	015
10	016	017	018	019	020	021	022	023	024	025	026	027	028	029	030	031
20	032	033	034	035	036	037	038	039	040	041	042	043	044	045	046	047
30	048	049	050	051	052	053	054	055	056	057	058	059	060	061	062	063
40	064	065	066	067	068	069	070	071	072	073	074	075	076	077	078	079
50	080	081	082	083	084	085	086	087	088	089	090	091	092	093	094	095
60	096	097	098	099	100	101	102	103	104	105	106	107	108	109	110	111
70	112	113	114	115	116	117	118	119	120	121	122	123	124	125	126	127
80	128	129	130	131	132	133	134	135	136	137	138	139	140	141	142	143
90	144	145	146	147	148	149	150	151	152	153	154	155	156	157	158	159
A0	160	161	162	163	164	165	166	167	168	169	170	171	172	173	174	175
B0	176	177	178	179	180	181	182	183	184	185	186	187	188	189	190	191
C0	192	193	194	195	196	197	198	199	200	201	202	203	204	205	206	207
D0	208	209	210	211	212	213	214	215	216	217	218	219	220	221	222	223
E0	224	225	226	227	228	229	230	231	232	233	234	235	236	237	238	239
F0	240	241	242	243	244	245	246	247	248	249	250	251	252	253	254	255

For conversion of larger numbers use the following in conjuction
with the table above.

Hexadecimal	Decimal
100	256
200	512
300	768
400	1024
500	1280
600	1536
700	1792
800	2048
900	2304
A00	2560
B00	2816
C00	3072
D00	3328
E00	3584
F00	3840
1000	4096
2000	8192
3000	12288
4000	16384
5000	20480
6000	24576
7000	28672
8000	32768
9000	36864
A000	40960
B000	45056
C000	49152
D000	53248
E000	57344
F000	61440

APPENDIX 4: *BASIC* INSTRUCTIONS USED

CALL "RESOLUTION" 0,2 sets the high resolution 320×192 graphics mode in basicsg2

CALL "PLOT" X,Y,N plots a graphics point at co-ordinates x,y with intensity N

CALL "LINE" X,Y,N displays a line beginning at the last plotted point to X,Y

CALL "CIRCLE" S,F,X,Y,N displays an arc of a circle radius 50 starting at S, ending at F at centre co-ordinates X,Y with intensity N

CLEAR N1,N2 clears memory space with start and finish memory addresses N1 and N2

POKE N1,N2 stores byte N2 in memory location N1

PEEK N1 fetches the byte stored in memory location N1

FOR I=N1 TO N2

.

.

NEXT I a loop which repeatedly executes the *BASIC* code between the FOR and NEXT instructions N2-N1 times

CREATE £10 opens a file to input data

CLOSE £10 closes the file

READ inputs the next item in the following DATA list

GOSUB N jumps to a subroutine, executes the

code there which with a RETURN instruction returns to the next numbered line in the main program

11. BIBLIOGRAPHY

RML <u>Research Machines 380Z Users' Guide</u>

Zilog <u>Z80 Programming Manual v2.0.</u> Pub. Mostek

Hutty, R. <u>Z80 Assembly Language Programming.</u> Pub. MacMillan

RML <u>Research Machines 380Z</u>

Zilog <u>Z80 CPU User Manual</u>

RML <u>Machine Language Programming Guide</u>

Alcock, D <u>Illustrating Basic .</u> Pub. CUP

Mircosoft <u>Microsoft Basic Reference Manual</u>

www.ingramcontent.com/pod-product-compliance
Lightning Source LLC
Chambersburg PA
CBHW071200050326
40689CB00011B/2191